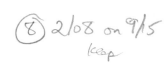

W9-BOM-970

© 2006

Praise for
The Three Hardest Words

"This book demonstrates that one of the seminal Christian thinkers in the postmodern era can also be a pastor. Leonard Sweet gets us to examine what it takes to live out love in this world, and he does it beautifully."

—TONY CAMPOLO, coauthor of *Adventures in Missing the Point* and professor of sociology at Eastern University

"Len Sweet has, in his inimitable style, tackled the three easiest-hardest words in the English language, wrestled them to the ground, hugged them, and then let them fly again. His imagination takes us on a journey, his mind is an encyclopedia of wonderful references, and his language is captivating. This book is a joy...and a challenge."

—TONY JONES, national coordinator of Emergent-US and author of *The Sacred Way*

"In *The Three Hardest Words*, Leonard Sweet plumbs the depths of Christianity to explore the richness of God's story, one that is abundant in love. As usual, Sweet's work is thought-provoking, insightful, and a must-read for any postmodern thinker."

—MARGARET FEINBERG, author of *Twentysomething* and *What the Heck Am I Going to Do with My Life?*

"Leonard Sweet has explored each of the 'three hardest words' in light of Scripture and God's kingdom. Journey with him to find out how God defines each of the words that sum up the Christian life: *I, love,* and *you.*"

—KIRBYJON CALDWELL, pastor, coauthor of *Entrepreneurial Faith,* and author of *The Gospel of Good Success*

"It turns out that Jesus' simplest and most basic command—that we are to love one another—is the hardest one for us to live out. Leonard Sweet's book is a tremendous help in guiding us not only to say the words 'I love you' with greater understanding of what they really mean, but also to live them with greater integrity and intention."

—RUTH HALEY BARTON, cofounder of the Transforming Center and author of *Sacred Rhythms*

"As corny as the song lyrics are, it's true that the world does need 'love sweet love.' But we need love the way Jesus expressed it. Len Sweet shows how to lose the cliché and make love a reality."

—DAN KIMBALL, pastor and author of *The Emerging Church* and *Emerging Worship*

"Leonard Sweet takes you on a journey out of yourself and into the transforming power of God's love. His fresh take on love can change your life and your community. Read, live, and breathe this provocative book."

—BEN YOUNG, pastor and author of *Out of Control: Finding Peace for the Physically Exhausted and Spiritually Strung Out*

THE THREE
HARDEST
WORDS

IN THE WORLD
TO GET RIGHT

THE THREE
HARDEST
WORDS

IN THE WORLD
TO GET RIGHT

LEONARD SWEET

WATERBROOK
PRESS

THE THREE HARDEST WORDS
PUBLISHED BY WATERBROOK PRESS
12265 Oracle Boulevard, Suite 200
Colorado Springs, Colorado 80921
A division of Random House Inc.

ISBN 1-57856-648-7

Library of Congress Cataloging-in-Publication Data
Sweet, Leonard I.
     The three hardest words in the world to get right / Leonard Sweet. — 1st ed.
          p. cm.
     Includes bibliographical references.
     ISBN 1-57856-648-7
     1. Christian life. 2. Love—Religious aspects—Christianity. I. Title.
     BV4501.3.S944 2006
     241'.4—dc22

                                                                                      2005033291

Printed in the United States of America
2006—First Edition

10 9 8 7 6 5 4 3 2 1

To Lynn and Jim Caterson
  Patrons
    Partners
      Participants in and Purveyors of The Presence

CONTENTS

ACKNOWLEDGMENTS

The writing of this book has lived up to its title: not only are these three words the hardest to get right, they've been for me the hardest to get written. If it had not been for Ron Lee, my editor at WaterBrook, this book never would have gotten out of the garage. When I stalled out, he pushed; when I ran out of gas, he refueled; when I broke down, he towed. I suspect every author who has worked with Ron is as grateful to WaterBrook as I am for bestowing the best on us.

My research assistant, Betty O'Brien, pulled off a tour de force in getting this book ready for Ron. The apostle Paul liked to say that "the love of Christ constrains [me]."[1] But I have found that the love of Christ confuses me as much as it constrains me. And while I was in various states of confusion, Betty kept her head and kept me steady. Her friendship is one of my life's greatest blessings.

This book was written mostly on the road. Just when I start getting discouraged at the declining quality of global travel, I think of traveling in the ancient world, which was even more uncomfortable, more dangerous, and enormously more time consuming. I don't know how Julius Caesar wrote a book during a lengthy crossing of the Alps, but I know I couldn't have written this one without the assistance of two Drew graduate students, Russ Wills and Karyn Wiseman.

I first tested out the manuscript on some DMin students at

George Fox University. Thanks to Denis Bell, Bryan Benjamin, Henry Berg, Ronald Coward, John Frank, Greg Glatz, Randall Groves, Joseph Kasio, Kerry McRoberts, Quintin Moore, Patrick Murunga, Patricia Oscarson, Lars Rood, Brian Ross, Christine Roush, Daniel Steigerwald, Jeffrey Tacklind, Fourie Van Den Berg, and Jacob Youmans.

"He didn't have much of a knack for living," a friend once said of Richard Yates. "Life had become an excuse for writing." Life can also become an excuse for consuming "stuff," or climbing ladders, or any number of things. But my temptation is clearly in the Yates direction. Without my family (Elizabeth, Len Jr., Justin, Thane, Soren, Egil) challenging my "excuses," I would keep forgetting that God is not going to ask me one day, "Sweet, how many books did you write?" In fact, it is my family's love and forgiveness that has taught me to live *The Message* version of 2 Corinthians 5:14: "Christ's love has moved me to such extremes. His love has the first and last word in everything we do."

Jim and Lynn Caterson were two of the very first people who believed in my ministry and lifted up my arms for ministry. They have been true Barnabas forces and trustworthy Aaron and Hur figures in my life.[2] I dedicate this book to them, and to their incarnation of "I-you love" in everything they do.

THE THREE
HARDEST
WORDS

IN THE WORLD
TO GET RIGHT

Life Cubed

When people know the end of their life is near, there are eleven words they most want to hear. According to a physician who has been present at the bedsides of too many dying patients to number, these are the words they most yearn for:

- "I'll miss you."
- "Thank you."
- "I forgive you."
- "I love you."

But if they could hear only one of these statements, they would choose "I love you."

This book explores the daily practice of that statement, which brings together life's three hardest words. These are the simple words that are the most difficult to get right: "I," "love," and "you."

What makes the words that everyone most wants to hear so hard to get right?

First, the greasy adolescent outpourings these three words frequently generate make each one of them slippery to pick up.

Second, human language fractures under the pressure these three words exert on it.

Third, each one of these words is essential to a biblical lifestyle, but each one has been corrupted by a culture that offers us a deathstyle, while calling it a "lifestyle." The divine-human relationship hinges on these three words and on the new identity, new integrity, and new intimacy that broke into history with the coming of the greatest Lover the world has ever known: Jesus the Christ. Jesus gave us a new way of being human. By living in The Presence, we now have "these three":

1. new identity of "I"
2. new integrity of "love"
3. new intimacy of "you"

Without identity, integrity, and intimacy, life is not truly life. Indeed life is death.

Jesus came to make sure we answer correctly two of the first questions God asked. In the beginning of Genesis God asked these questions:

- *"Where are you?"*[1] This question, directed to Adam and Eve, is the most universal question of existence: Where in the world are you? Where are you in the world? I call it the Identity Question.

- *"Where is your brother?"*[2] Our sin and our shame echo with the answer: "Am I my brother's keeper?" I call this question, which as Cain realized is really two questions wrapped in one, the Integrity and Intimacy Question.

> Loving one's neighbour is the birth act of humanity.
>
> — SOCIOLOGIST ZYGMUNT BAUMAN[3]

"THESE THREE..."

Part of the magic of "I Love You" is found not only in each individual word but also in their triplicity. "These three" is a phrase that constantly occurs in the New Testament, and for good reason. For the Christian everything is cubed. Not squared, cubed. The kingdom of God is a cubed community. Christianity is a cubist spirituality.

> Go therefore and make disciples of all nations,
> baptizing them in the name of the Father
> and of the Son and of the Holy Spirit.
>
> — MATTHEW 28:19

Life moves in threes. Bad news and good news travel in packs of three. Love comes in a triadic package.

Three is the most sacred number in Jewish-Christian history. It is the symbol of union, completion, and perfection. The times of daily prayer were three.[4] The sanctuary had three divisions.[5] Both the Tabernacle and the Temple consisted of three parts, and the Holy of Holies was a cube. Three angels appeared to Abraham and Sarah at the oaks of Mamre,[6] the first proleptic of the Blessed Trinity: "One God in Three Persons." Three days and nights Jonah was buried in the belly of the huge fish.[7] Three is the organizational structure of The Lord's Prayer, according to Lorraine Kisly's lyrical exploration of the Our Father. Her literal translation of the Greek makes the prayer an action plan for daily living:

> Come, the kingdom of you
> Be done, the will of you...
> Be manifest, the glory of you.[8]

On three things the World [or Age] stands:
on the Torah, on the [Temple] service,
and on deeds of lovingkindness.

—SIMEON THE JUST (CA. 350–200 BC)[9]

Three is also the survival number. You can go only three seconds without blood, three minutes without air, three days without water, three weeks without food. Jesus asked only one person, "Do you love me?" And he asked him three times over breakfast. Three chances are what Jesus gave Peter to answer the same question, and Jesus made Peter repeat the answer three times to make sure Peter got it.

Three is the bad-to-good number. No matter how bad things are now, no matter how many troubles you may think you have, "wait three days" before doing anything drastic. Three days is how long it took for the worst day in the history of the world (Good Friday) to turn into the best day in the history of the world (Easter Sunday).

Three is the leadership number. The distance between a martyr and a leader? Three paces. The leading edge is three paces behind the bleeding edge. The threshold of three reminds us that there is such a thing as one oddness too many. There's an old saying, "He that thinketh he leadeth but hath no one following is only taking a walk."[10] Leadership is a blend of three forces: leaders, followers, and systems. Leaders need an inner circle of three confidants and confederates: Jesus had "The Three" (the "advanced" disciples, Peter, James, and John). Leadership stories bring together three narratives: the leader's story, the community's story, and the contextual story.

Holy, holy, holy
is the Lord God Almighty,
who was, and is, and is to come.

—REVELATION 4:8, NIV

Three is the number of perfection.

- three critiques (Kant)
- three dialectics to history (Hegel)
- three states of matter: solid, liquid, gas
- three kinds of thinking: serial, associative, and unitive
- three levels of the self: ego, id, and superego
- three testaments: First Testament, Second Testament, Third Testament (your life as a disciple of Jesus; your life as the fifth gospel)
- three transcendentals of being: beauty, truth, goodness

Made in the image of God, humans too are trinity: body, spirit, soul! The wisdom of the whole comes when all three are working together in harmony.

Never buy an antique until you can find three things wrong with it. That's what proves its antiquity and makes it "the perfect antique." Even the very best flaws come in threes.

Want a perfect day? Don't forget the 3 percent rule: 3 percent of the population is absolutely bonkers, total zanies, even sociopathic. In other words, 3 percent of the people you will encounter every day are loony-toons. You can't judge the 97 percent by the 3 percent, or let the 3 percent ruin the day for you. Most major crime is perpetrated by an amazingly small number of people. Some fifty thousand people out of a USAmerica population of nearly 296 million commit about 90 percent of all burglaries, for example.[11] Some people are just born bad—or more accurately, badder than the rest of us.

There are *three* offices of Christ that show his perfection: Prophet, Priest, and King. The total triumph of Jesus in his temptation is his threefold use of "It is written!" *Three* times God the Father spoke from heaven to the Son, showing God's perfect pleasure in the Son's obedience and completeness in carrying out God's mission in the world.[12]

Author and leadership consultant Robert Dale describes how storytellers use what he calls the "rule of three" to "unfold tales and truth to us for ages."

> We see this pattern in Scripture. Abraham, Isaac, and Jacob. Father, Son, and Holy Spirit. Prodigal son, waiting father, and unhappy elder son.... Priest, Levite, and Good Samaritan on the Jericho Road.... The same device of triplicity is common in secular stories, advertising, and in world history as well. Tom, Dick and Harry. The three little pigs, the three blind mice, the three Stooges. Small, medium, large. Snap, crackle, pop. Green, yellow, red traffic lights. The good, bad, and ugly. 'I came, I saw, I conquered' announced Caesar of the Pontic campaign. Beginning, middle, and end.[13]

Three is the relationship number. Protodownscaler Henry David Thoreau said he had only three chairs: "one for solitude, two for friendship, three for society."[14] In Acts 26:9 Paul admitted, "I thought to myself" and found out that it was too small a committee. He explains: "I myself once thought it my duty to work actively against the name of Jesus."[15] I cannot know myself all by myself. It takes three to know one.

Three is the magic multiplying number:

- Three times three ranks of bodiless creatures: nine Cherubim, Seraphim, and Thrones; Dominions, Virtues, and Powers; Principalities, Archangels, and Angels.
- Three times three months: ninety days is the approximate length of most sports seasons. Ninety days is the time you've got to get something started or forget doing it.
- Three times one generation (of forty years): one hundred twenty years is the maximum human life span.[16] One hundred twenty years is basically how long God designed the human body to last without augmentation.
- Three times ten: thirty is the maximum number for organic cells. Anything beyond this will move the group from relational to formal, from organic to organized.
- Three times one hundred: three hundred is the maximum size of a church that one pastor can personally care for. The three hundred barrier is the invisible ceiling for "congregational" churches—as Gideon himself discovered.

Even without multiplication, the meaning and impact of three is impressive. Christ was crucified at the third hour. The inscription over his head was written in three languages, suggesting humanity's complete, global rejection of Christ. On the third day he rose from the dead.

Three persons were raised from the dead by Jesus: Jairus's daughter, the widow's son, and Lazarus. Jesus exercised his divine life-giving power in all three stages of human existence: The First Age—the daughter of Jairus was twelve years old, just a girl; The Second Age—the son of the widow of Nain was of adult age, a young man; The Third Age—Lazarus was full grown, an old man.

The church is a "cubed" community, a place where all relationships, all interactions, all prayers, and all decisions are carried out with the power of three. And the power of three is best expressed in the cubed language of love: "I love you," which are the three hardest words in the world to get right. If we get these three words wrong, we are guilty of "under-understanding" (in the words of Ronald Rolheiser) and "under-living" (in the words of Walter Brueggemann) the amazing "immensity" of the gospel.[17]

Get these three words right and you cube everything you do with power. Draw on the power of these three words and the blocks that lock the secrets of the universe start to open. But we will never get "I love you" right unless we first get the *story* of love right. Without the right love story, we have no hope of living in the authentic Identity, Integrity, and Intimacy of "I love you."

PART I

THE UNIVERSAL
LOVE STORY

1

THE DIFFERENCE
BETWEEN LIFE
AND LIFESTYLE

Meaning in Life Doesn't Mean What It Used To

On life's path, not to advance
is to go backward, for nothing
that exists remains immobile.
—SAINT BERNARD

All around us a new way of living has developed. The irony is that it's actually a new way of dying. Thus, a new way of life is being born in reverse.

What does it mean? Every age is pregnant with possibilities. But only a few ages move beyond pregnancy to the nursery. Such momentous times give birth to new ways of living and moving and being in the world.[1] Since the mid-1960s, a new species of humanity, homo postmoderns, has appeared. British poet Philip Larkin (1922–1985) was right: the world did change in 1963, "Between the end of the Chatterley ban/And the Beatles' first LP."[2] Look at the Beatles' first record album or watch any Elvis movie from 1963. From that moment on, any attempt to establish a canon, whether of musical taste or of metaphysical truth, was doomed to philosophical and cultural ridicule.[3]

We usually associate hope with birth. But what are we to conclude from the new ways of "living" that are being birthed in our current age? The title *Apocalypse Now* is best known for a movie about the Vietnam War. But it is an even better name for the times in which we are living. The word *apocalypse* literally means "revela-

> I think that a lot of things in our society are moving away from communicating in words toward a way that I don't understand, toward the visual—and some of it I think is very good—but it's a world I don't know.
>
> —CANADIAN POET MARGARET AVISON (B. 1918)[4]

tion, an uncovering of what has been hidden." But a more nuanced understanding of the word means less "the end of the world" than "the end of the world as we've known it" and the beginning of a whole new world of human existence.[5] Life and familiar ways of living—and even the meaning we usually associate with life and lifestyle—no longer adhere to the expected norm. Meaning in life doesn't mean what it used to.

Every institution in society is undergoing a massive restructuring, rebirth, and reorienting.[6] If you doubt this is true, here are two quick examples. The church you attended as a child—if you attended one—would be completely out of step with daily life experience today. If the church you were part of back then has refused to be reborn and reoriented, then it is indeed out of place or out of existence. The live-wire early twentieth-century mainline church, which confidently named the twentieth century "The Christian Century," is now in the dock or is dead wood.[7] The unspoken echo of "Saturday Night Live" is "Sunday Morning Dead."

For a second example: Think about the way you do your work today. No workplace has stayed the same over the past thirty years.

- When Bill Clinton assumed the presidency in 1993, the World Wide Web boasted only fifty sites.[8]
- Today, when you disconnect from the Internet, you feel like you just pulled the plug on a loved one.
- China now has more Internet users than any other nation.[9] Three-fourths of all South Korean households boast a high-speed Internet connection, while only 18 percent of US households do.[10]

- In the "Chinafication" of the world's economy, productivity is nearly 20 percent higher in China than in leading European countries and almost as high as in the US. China now consumes 40 percent of the world's cement, a third of its coal, and a quarter of its steel.
- The first computer I worked with wasn't a box, it was a room. By 2015, new computer memories composed of nanoparticles will contain in digital format the entire contents of the Library of Congress in a machine the size of a yo-yo.
- Buy a Dell computer these days and it will probably have been assembled at an airport near you by FedEx employees out of components shipped from companies around the world. Dell itself doesn't touch the things that land on your doorstep.
- The clothes we buy come from China, our cars from Japan, fruits and vegetables from South America, and luxury goods from Europe. When we call for tech support, the person at the other end of the line is more likely to be in India than in Indiana.[11]
- At least one-fifth of the adult working population works at least one day a week from home, on the road, at a tele-work center, or at a satellite office.[12] These numbers are mushrooming.
- In 1960, 70 percent of American women between the ages of twenty and twenty-four were married; by 2000 the number had dropped to 27 percent.[13]

- In 1970 there were only ten non-Catholic megachurches in the US; in 2004 there were 835, and growing.[14]

If you could choose what age to be born in, what would you choose? No matter how much we would love to sit at the feet of Jesus or discuss theology at Martin Luther's table or be nurtured in the faith by Susanna Wesley or walk the streets of Selma with Martin Luther King Jr. or accompany Mother Teresa on the streets of Calcutta, we have no alternative but to choose to live in the twenty-first century, and not to blanche when asked to bear witness in the midst of it all. The hands of Providence have placed us where we are most needed.

> One place comprehended can make us understand other places better.
>
> —NOVELIST EUDORA WELTY[15]

The next three decades may well be the most epochal in human history. For the kind of world being born will depend on us—our grasp of where we have come from and our reach for where we are going. How does the church respond to such a time as this? How does the church lead in such a time as this? How can we help the church have 20/20 vision…and beyond? It will be up to us—both individually and collectively, both as leaders and as followers—to hear God and see what God is doing and then to join in.

The key word here is not "join" but "join in." It's more than a matter of "joining" a church. It's not about getting people to choose to join what a church is doing. It's about getting people to join in what God is already doing.[16] The Bible is less a book about what we are to do than a book about what God has already done and is now doing, and how we can join in God's "doings." Without taking ourselves too seriously, are we prepared to take God's mission very seriously?

When the history of Pearl Harbor was written, it was titled *At Dawn We Slept.*[17] Let it not be said of us that we were no-shows to the future.

LET'S TALK ABOUT THE ELEPHANT IN THE ROOM

Perhaps the defining characteristic of "the end of the world as we've known it" is the so-called "death of the metanarrative." In every discussion of postmodernity, it is the ghost at the feast, the elephant in

> Nothing stands up,
> nothing stands clear and whole,
> Everything bits and pieces.
>
> —ANTHONY THWAITE[18]

the room. No one can completely avoid it, but no one wants to fully acknowledge it either.

To embrace the word *metanarrative* is like naming your child Ebola or Ecoli or Osama. What is it about the idea of a metanarrative that creates so many problems for so many people?

Metanarrative literally means a master narrative, a "grand story," but in the modern world that is now ending, the "meta" was long on "grand" and short on "story." It was much more a Big Point or a Big Principle, or even a Big Rule, than it was a Big Picture or Big Story. The modern-era metanarrative assured people there were universal claims and grand foundational principles on which life could be safely built and securely grounded. Learn the principle, keep it in mind at all times, live accordingly, and you'll have it made. No need to grapple with complexity and paradox—just feel free to overlook all the things that violate and seem to disprove the foundational principle. After all, it's the principle that really counts, not any transcendent story that might give real meaning to your life. Rather than providing a story that would engage the imagination and stir the spirit, the modern era gave us a grand rule that promised false security and empty "success." What is more, when postmoderns hear the word *metanarrative,* they hear at the same time the low hum of sexism and racism playing in the background.

In postmodern culture, however, stories are important. It is inviolable principles that are suspect. Or, more carefully stated, in postmodern culture *personal* stories are okay. But not totalizing or cosmic stories that cross religious, historical, or cultural boundaries. The eye of the beholder has replaced the eye of eternity, since the subspecie *aeternitatis* type of metanarrative smacks too gamely of the modern-era reliance on ironclad principles and bottom-line universal truths, rather than the narrowed, personal narrative that might provide some context for the chaos in one's life. On Monday, Wednesday, and Friday we believe the believable. And on Tuesday, Thursday, and Saturday we believe.

The loss of modern-era assurances of security and safety has wreaked havoc on the human soul. In fact, it has led to a rebirth of the ancient gods and goddesses—Gaea, Hermes, Hera, Prometheus, Dionysus—who are returning to rule planet Earth with a vengeance. Their reappearance is veiled because they are not returning as religions but as live-and-let-live lifestyle choices. In the cult of commodified lifestylism, even religion has become one more box on the shelf—promising a personal benefit along with conditioning shampoo, long-lasting antiperspirant, breath-sweetening toothpaste, low-fat salad dressing, extended-wear contact lenses, and 724 different fruits and vegetables. If gods are whatever you worship, we are all polytheists now.[19]

The Two Choices

With the commodification of personal spirituality, two major "lifestyle choices" have filled the vacuum left by the loss of metanarrative. The primary belief system that governs the globe is the marriage of Croesus (money) and Hedone (pleasure). Mexican novelist Carlos Fuentes has dubbed this form of materialist lifestylism "cresohedonic" consumerism.[20] If you doubt the hold that cresohedonic lifestylism has on the human psyche, take a poll of entering freshmen at Harvard or Princeton on why they worked so hard to get there. Wisdom and the love of learning take a back seat to the quest for power,[21] privilege, and pleasure. Or check out the rapid growth of residential communities known as "common interest developments" (CIDs), which cater to people seeking a particular lifestyle (golf, boating, singles).

> ## If we don't do what we want we're not Divine.
>
> —THE SIXTIES BEAT ETHOS[22]

If cresohedonic consumerism wants to be as fresh as wet paint, the other current lifestyle choice wants to be as solid as nails. The second prevailing belief system is fundamentalist idealism. Postmodern culture is home to a cornucopia of fundamentalisms—back-to-nature fundamentalisms, Green or Gaia fundamentalisms, alternative-medicine fundamentalisms, civil-religion fundamentalisms, biblical fundamentalisms (whether the holy book be the Torah, the Koran, or the Bible), even humanist fundamentalisms. Secular humanism is best described as one form of religious humanism, since it can be as fundamentalist and zealous as any right-wing religious or political fundamentalism. In its arrogance, secular humanism sees all religious faith as an irrational burp, something to be hushed at best and suppressed at worst (whether by tissue or treatment).

What distinguishes each fundamentalism is less its intolerance or irrationality[23] than its crabbed and crabby vision of the future. An attempt to control the future dominates every fundamentalism. Fundamentalists are people who think they can say "Stop the world; I want to get off" to a world "already in progress."[24] A yearning for yesteryear, a hankering after the palmy days of the past, a nostalgia for what never did happen, is at the heart of fundamentalism. The Bible challenges us to "remember the days of old," to honor the "years of many generations," but not to live in them. Alpha and Omega are yoked, but Alpha is not Omega.[25]

People have separated into two groups. On one side they have nostalgically clung to the old world of solid foundations while raging at the age that is emerging. On the other, they have free-fallen into a world of absent absolutes and lost centers with little lament or backward looks, all the while singing "follow your bliss" and buying every bling-bling excess that floats their boats. The first path leads to rigor mortis of the soul. The second leads to timor mortis. You can hear no aria of the human soul in either.

Subtext over Grand Text

The author may be dead, so the joke on postmodernism goes, but the publisher still knows where to send the royalty checks. The metanarrative may no longer work, but megamalls and shopping bags are still alive and kicking in ever-greater kicks. Just as no one worries about setting his or her laptop on the table after the physicist says furniture is mostly empty space on an atomic level, so people don't worry about life's being a sham just because the metanarrative that makes life whole has curdled in the postmodern air, where "every point of view is just a view from a point."

Today, people of most any stripe readily reject a grand narrative that asserts absolute authority, anything that would claim to be binding beyond this life. But a small story, now *there's* something we can sink our teeth into. And the secularized religions of commodified spirituality offer hosts of small stories that all peter out in a trail of dot-dot-dot... How many fast-food restaurants now serve yogurt and fruit, tossed salads, and low-carb menu items based on the millions of Americans who follow the absolute dictates of best-selling diet books? Small stories are not only credible, they are capable of changing the lives and commerce of millions. But at the same time, the grand narrative has fallen into disfavor.

> Underneath western culture runs an enormous, ancient, linear story we dimly sense, a story that starts with an imperative sentence in an omniscient voice: Let there be light.
>
> —SOUTHERN NOVELIST DORIS BETTS[26]

This shift in which our subtexts are larger than our master texts leaves us not with a new or improved approach to life but only a temporary and ultimately fatalistic preamble to death. It's a choice we make to turn our backs on the glimmers of transcendence on earth in favor of a temporary pleasure feast enjoyed prior to dying. As a result, we have entered an era in which death—or dying by inches—is somehow more appealing than life and transcendence. We have rejected the metanarrative that helps give form and substance to life (and even to life beyond this life) in order to embrace the small narratives of false idols, consumerism, and self-indulgence that promise short-term bliss and lead ultimately to death.

What Makes the Narrative So Grand

If the metanarrative is about anything, it's about life. And more specifically, it's about love as the form and function of life. To put life and love in their necessary context, the metanarrative tells us not only who we are, but also who everyone else is—helping us understand and live well in relationship with the "other." The grand narrative, which has fallen into disfavor in so many quarters, has much to show us about ourselves, the meaning of love, and those around us. It is the story of "I love you" like no other love story.

It's time to reexamine what we have lost with the discarding of the grand narrative, the underlying story of all of life.

2

WHEN A LIFESTYLE IS REALLY A DEATHSTYLE

God's Story as the Unifying Theory of Everything

> Not everything that counts
> can be counted.
> —A SIGN IN ALBERT EINSTEIN'S
> OFFICE AT PRINCETON

A company known as G. W. Little, which stages fashion shows for dogs, offers to accessorize your "pamper-worthy pooch" with the latest fashion accessory: the Diva Dogbone Necklace.

A stunning double strand of 8mm freshwater cultured lavender and cream colored pearls. The "bone" accents are 14K white gold and…they're pave set with round brilliant cut diamonds and pink sapphires! Diamonds have a combined total weight of approximately 0.10cts. Sapphires are combined 1.05cts. Each piece is hand-made and strung on plastic coated steel cable for strength and durability. The clasp is also 14K white gold pave set "bone." Comes in a high-polish mahogany box with white leatherette inserts and pillow.[1]

For $1,995 (higher for large dogs), G. W. Little will gladly put your dog on the cutting edge of canine fashion. But the company promises to do even more. It specializes in "Lifestyles for the Little Dog." Clearly, this goes *way* beyond simply supplying luxurious jewelry for your favorite pet.

> There are no absolutes, and I'll have my three eggs over easy, with a side of bacon and biscuits. Everything is relative, and put the Diva Dogbone Necklace on my credit card, please.

High-cost and high-gloss pet accouterments represent just one category within the prevailing commercial entities of today—companies that market not products or services, but a different life. Product lines have been supplanted by the sale of new lifestyles. No longer do you buy breakfast cereal or go to get your hair done—you buy into a superior life. Or at least that is what is promised.

Def Jam is known for its records and hip-hop artists (Kanye West, Ne-Yo, Ludacris, Rihanna, 112, DMX, Young Jeezy). But Def Jam is more than a recording company. "For twenty years, we've not only been making music, but building a lifestyle.... We never felt we were a record company. We always felt we were a lifestyle company. And if you wanna be the cool kid, then you wanna have access to Def Jam Mobile services and whatever we're providing."[2]

> We don't sell appliances, we sell lifestyles.
>
> —ONE-TIME SLOGAN OF APPLIANCE COMPANY BRAUN

It's easy to feel smug and superior when you compare yourself to pet lovers who waste two thousand dollars on a dog collar or when you scoff at white suburban kids who buy into the false hype of the hip-hop lifestyle. But it will not do to insult such people by telling them they need to "get a life," or that their luxe life exudes nothing but shallowness and lack of meaning. The truth is just the opposite. The ancient gods of pleasure and power offer life stories full of plot and purpose. In very real terms, if you buy into this secular religion, a large part of what you are buying into is "meaning." Ask the nine hundred guests of the Bellagio in Las Vegas who on an average day visit its spa, getting treatments as diverse as Thai yoga massage, gem therapy, Indian head massage, Balinese massage, and an Egyptian gold treatment in which "real gold is dusted on the face and body leaving the guest ready for a dazzling night on the town."[3]

The notion that non-Christians have no meaning, and that everyone outside the faith needs to "get a life," is a prevailing assumption among Christians. But it is wrongheaded and self-serving for Christians to assume that they are the only people on the planet who have meaning. Listen to the dean of Yale's environmental school, who has spent a lifetime fighting for the environment:

> Consumption brings us pleasure and helps us to avoid pain and, worst of all, boredom and monotony. Consumption is stimulating, diverting, absorbing, defining, empowering, relaxing, fulfilling, educational, rewarding. If pressed, I would have to confess that I truly enjoy most of the things on which I spend money.[4]

If money can't buy you happiness, you're probably shopping at the wrong stores.

The USAmerican Dream, revered even by most Christians, contradicts the notion that the religions of the ancient gods reap a harvest of nothing more than loneliness and a louche life. The *old* USAmerican Dream of a good job, a nice house, two-point-five kids, and two cars has morphed into the *new* USAmerican Dream where joy and fulfillment come from work you can play at, play that works for a lifetime, and two places to live that are filled with family and friends with whom you can share experiences of fine dining, travel, entertainment, and personal health. Buying satisfaction in life is no longer a process of accumulating the most things, but a journey of seeking the best and most meaningful experiences with the things and services you buy. Whether in its old or newer versions, the USAmerican Dream has built one of the most commercially successful civilizations in the history of planet Earth. It would be almost impossible to prove the case that none of this has created some form of meaning for its devotees. And for many the false meaning of "lifestylism" is more powerful and indeed more "meaning-full" than the rote, principle-based, secure religion of modern Christianity.

When many outsiders look at the "lifestyle choice" of Christians, who spend their lives sitting in the same pew, singing the same songs, reciting the same words, smiling at the same people, listening to the same thoughts, and building bigger barns that all look the same, they scratch their heads in wonderment that anyone in her right mind would choose that kind of "life."

> ## The Best Surprise Is No Surprise
>
> —HOLIDAY INN SLOGAN

It is not that people (and even Christian people) don't have a life. It's that they don't have a true life, an abundant life as Jesus defined both "abundance" and "life." They have not allowed God to stretch their human imagination beyond conventional categories. The explanation for this incredible loss of true life? The metanarrative of God has been cast aside in an odd trade for safe principles and a controllable life with bubble-bath dreams.

SIMPLY LIVING, OR EXPERIENCING LIFE?

As we get caught up in living, it is all too easy for "life" to never quite start. Like birds that live trapped inside an airport terminal, our lives are full and free, even bountiful. It's just that the real world waits outside. It's the difference between building your nest in a ponderosa pine and building your nest in a Starbucks sign.

In some cases it's less a matter of having a false lifestyle and more that we have a death lifestyle. Every day we choose life or death, and many choose death. Everyday life, as rich and rewarding as it is, sometimes is not really an everyday "life" at all. It is an everyday death.[5] We rush through life never really living on this planet except

> Whaling will end only when the whalers can find no more whales.
>
> —JEREMY CHERFAS[6]

as the dinosaurs lived on it. A dinosaurian philosophy of life is a basic brain response to everyday existence: feed on this, fight about that, protect yourself, and pleasure yourself as often as possible. And like the dinosaurs with their four rules of living—feeding, fighting, fleeing, and sex—we bring death and destruction to all around us as we ravage and ruin whatever we touch.

Shortly after the prehistoric paintings of bison were discovered in the caves of Lascaux, France, the images began to vanish. The carbon dioxide from the hoards of visitors to the caves (twelve hundred per day in the mid-1950s) were disintegrating the paint.[7] The more beautiful something is (for example, the French Riviera), the more we humans will destroy it. We can't leave it alone, and the dinosaurian ways of modern mastodons have unleashed a reverse Midas touch on nature: everything we finger turns to dross.

SMALLER THAN LIFE

If you consider their long-term impact on people and the planet, the ancient gods of power, wealth, and pleasure offer more a deathstyle than a lifestyle, a smaller-than-life way of living in the world that aluminums (rather than illumines) the mind, blocks (rather than arterializes) the heart, and over time, asphyxiates the soul. When all is said and done, when the ancient gods reign, nothing is said and done. The lifestyle choices of too many people (including too many Christians) lead nowhere and end up nowhere.

So why isn't the church shouting the truth in the face of the gods' deathstyle? Why have we become the silent people sitting in pews with prayer stares? Why isn't the church sounding the loudest warning: "That way boredom and death lies!"

The preference for deathstyle over lifestyle continues to spread. And while Christians should be sounding the alarm, we also can learn from people who make other lifestyle choices. For example, I stand in rapt amazement that some of the most courageous people I know are atheists. The Bible says that our "labor is not in vain."[8] To face the future with the bare-knuckled belief that one labors in vain; to get up every day knowing that one's life has no eternal significance; to warm the shivering soul with the mantle of relativism—that takes a level of courage that few Christians can match outside of Polycarp at the pyre, Ignatius at the coliseum, Hus at the scaffold, Tyndale stewing in his own juices, Archbishop Oscar Romero at the bullet-riddled altar.

But there are virtues higher than courage. For example, the virtues of faith and trust in God. There are pursuits higher than happiness. For example, pursuit of the kingdom of God. There are dreams higher than NASA's domains. For example, "slipping the surly bonds"[9] of earth-bound thinking and putting on the mind of Christ.

REVISITING THE GRAND NARRATIVE

As noted earlier, the idea of a metanarrative has fallen out of fashion. It is thought that no one story can give meaning to the world's vast variety of people, tribes, beliefs, and preferences. Better to allow each group—and even each individual—its own narrative, so that meaning is found much closer to home, much closer to one's own experience.

But to opt for a narrative du jour or narrative à la mode is a life-cheating exchange. To live as Jesus lived, and as God dreams we will live today, we need nothing else more than we need a metanarrative that situates our own story writing within the Big Story. Some people are born early risers. Others rise to the occasion. We need both. Some people write their life story in prose, others in poetry. We need both. Some people bring less peace than they do the sword. We need both. But all stories need to stew together in the same pot.

When we lose the stories that give life coherence, we have lost everything. The world that is emerging today needs a master narrative more than ever; the great need is for something that offers people more than "lifestyle choices." Literary critic Walter Benjamin may have been right when he complained seventy years ago that "the epic side of truth, wisdom, is dying out."[10] But that need not mean that the day of the grand story is over, or that the art of storytelling is nearing its end. If "the epic side of truth" is in decline, the rise of a "grand story" is all the more imperative.

Why Christians should have succumbed to the postmodern mantra that the day of the grand narratives is over, when some of the loudest voices in our world are offering competing "grand stories" and totalitarian visions, is a whole other story.[11] If you look around, it's impossible *not* to see our age's big stories.

Al Qaeda is designing a Big Picture and putting it on display around the world. And engineer Osama bin Laden, pediatrician

Ayman al-Zawahiri, and architect-planner Mohamed Atta have reserved a place for *you* in that Big Picture.

Burger King has a Whopper on hand around the world. And the franchised "have it your way" philosophy is grabbed daily by millions under golden crowns and Arcos Dorados (the golden arches).

Hollywood has a Big Screen reeling 'round the clock. And its celebrity cult of fame and fashion, working in partnership with Madison Avenue and Rodeo Drive, wants to draw you forever into its glistening darkness.

Political novelist Salman Rushdie has a crusade going for the universal truth of "universal rights" based on being a "human." Known for celebrating hybridization and cultural mongrelization in his books (he also collaborated with U2 on the song "The Ground Beneath Her Feet"),[12] Rushdie at the same time advocates the notion that human beings, by virtue of their being (not their cultural background) have certain inalienable rights.[13] Rushdie argues that cultural relativism, or the notion that certain things are simply local cultural constructs and not universal truths, is a dangerous idea. In other words, just because your culture condones killing doesn't mean you should be free to kill. Just because your culture advocates cannibalism doesn't mean you should feel free to eat human flesh.

Among novelists such as Reynolds Price, Richard Russo, and Toni Morrison, the omniscient point of view and metanarrator is a favorite way to tell one or more of the seven basic story lines of human existence.[14] Likewise, scientists such as Stephen Hawking haven't given up on a metanarrative. Beginning with Albert Einstein, scientists have pursued an ultimate "theory of everything" (TOE) that would wrap up the universe in one elegant package. Superstring theory is the most recent attempt to fulfill Einstein's dream of a single, all-embracing theory of the universe, a unified theory of all the forces in physics. Science is more enamored than ever of a "grand story."

CLAMORING FOR A GRAND METANARRATIVE

The need for a "grand metanarrative" is greater than ever, in spite of widespread opposition to the idea that any one narrative is capable of guiding all people in all cultures for all time. The following are four reasons why we need to return to a master narrative.

1) To Combat Fragmentation

In this increasingly globalized world, we need the countervailing centripetal force of a grand narrative that can pull us together in the face of all the centrifugal forces that would rip us apart. In the words of theologian Nicholas Lash, "Globalization requires us to try to tell a story in which 'the world' refers to everything, and in which 'we' refers to the whole of humankind."[15] More than ever, the entire world needs to be brought into a single global discourse about its common heritage and its common destiny. The hopes and dreams of the merchant farmer in Fallujah and the machinist in Detroit are not all that different. But without a global metanarrative that arises out of a common conversation, our ignorance and fear prevent us from understanding that we all want the same things: secure and flourishing futures for our children, and the touch of transcendence for those we love.

Of course, as Lash goes on to admit, "No story says everything, not even a story of everything!"[16] That's why the Grand Story will end up being always "stories of everything," with as many different versions of the one Grand Story as there are indigenous cultures and tribes. The metanarrative of The Presence can be entered at many points and unfolds through many narrative lines. There is one gospel, many cultures. There is *not* one gospel, one culture. The universality of Christ does not cancel the particularity of Jesus, and vice versa. Jesus is the "concrete universal."[17] That is why the public voice of Christianity must always be a chorus of voices.

The Hebrew tradition has a saying: "The Torah is One, but it has seventy faces." A variant version of this saying is "The Torah is one, but it has six hundred thousand faces" (referring to the number present when the Torah was revealed). Each person receives and lives the One Torah a bit differently, depending on each one's unique attributes and abilities.[18] But however many voices are singing, and in however many different parts of harmony, the song is the same.

The differences among us are part of the pleasure, not the problem. There is a theology of Paul, a theology of Luke, a theology of John, a theology of Mark. There are four gospels, but one Jesus.

2) To Cultivate Faith with a Future Orientation

What you think of when you hear that word *global* depends on whether you think of globalization as golden beaches or golden arches.[19] The Western church's "globalphobia," as one scholar puts it,[20] has something to do with being terrified of our world but even more to do with being terrified of the future. We pay lip service to the future but don't seem to be able to think future or live in light of the future.

> [Jesus] went on ahead, going
> up to Jerusalem.
>
> LUKE 19:28

The Christian metanarrative takes place in three time zones simultaneously (past, present, future). But because the "universe is organically resting on—cantilevered on, I might say—the future as its sole support," as Teilhard de Chardin memorably put it,[21] the future is the major time zone in which Christian faith has its being. As Jesus always goes ahead of us, just as Jesus came to Peter and the disciples from way out on the water, we must be open to a God who comes to us from the future, encouraging us to catch up.

God's love story—the tale of "I love you"—has a future face. The biblical metanarrative bears a future fingerprint. The essence of vocation is "call," which implies a future orientation. To be "called" is to be drawn forward, away from where you are and toward where God wants you to be, toward "the hope to which [God] has called you."[22] The name for church in the New Testament is *ecclesia*, which literally means the "called-out ones." The church is called out of holy huddles to run downfield into the future. Leadership is the art, not primarily of reaching people where they are, but of reaching people where they are *not*—but where God is calling them to be. You can call this class Quarterback 101, where a "leader" learns that the key to a successful forward pass is throwing the ball, not to where the receiver is, but to where the receiver is going to be.

One of Paul's key words is *prothumos,* which we translate as "eager" or "ready" or "prepared." But the word also means "to think with a future mind."[23] Paul learned to think with a future mind after the Damascus Road experience, where he was not given a road map to the future or a blueprint for his "calling." Rather, he was told to "go" and face the future head on, with all its uncertainty and unknowns, for only then "You will be told what you are to do."[24] No wonder, regardless of how many New Testament letters were up Paul's sleeve, they were all cuffed by this one link: "Today we remember tomorrow."

In the master-narratives of Christian history, precedence is given to the future over the past. They carry with them what poet Tom Paulin calls, in a title to one of his poems, "nostalgia for the future."[25] In the biblical metanarrative, the expression "you're history" needs to mean not "you're toast" but you're a part of making history, of forging the future, of shaping The Presence on earth. The future is made from the facts of history, and there is no bigger fact than *you*. God has given you a calling, and the direction of your calling is always into the future.

This "today we remember tomorrow" faith is not easy, and postmodern culture is not making it any easier. Everything is moving at such warp speed that memory does not have time to settle and embed an identity. People are dazed by change, mazed by choice, dazzled by life's "foundations" being swept away by one cultural tsunami after another. This makes the need for a metanarrative that focuses on the future without leaving the past or present behind all the more pressing. In the words of Yale theologian Miroslav Volf:

> "My sense is that contemporary culture does not have this
> notion of a definite future toward which we are headed,
> but rather an empty concept of perpetual novelty has
> replaced a stable and morally filled concept of the future....
> The resultant feeling is like driving a fast-moving car on a
> highway. Our experience of life is a blur—not stable
> images, integrated into a larger framework of meaning."[26]

Think about these words: "I feel alone." This is the telling statement made by John Walker Lindh. Raised a Roman Catholic in an affluent California home where he was taught he was free to find and define himself, Lindh decided to become a hip-hop star. He even posed in Internet chat rooms as a black hip-hop artist who railed against capitalism, globalization, homosexuality, the fakeness of Christianity, and the falsity of Zionism. Fearful of the future, buffeted by constant change, and unable to "find himself" on his own, he escaped to the well-defined grooves of fundamentalist Islam. After studying with a mullah in Pakistan, he joined the Taliban as Abdul Hamid the freedom fighter and battled the USAmericans in Afghanistan. "In the U.S. I feel alone," he confessed. "Here I feel comfortable and at home."[27]

The real Christian view of the future is unblinkingly bifocal: the future is where you go...to die; the future is where you go...to make dreams come true. Because of the resurrection metanarrative, Christians can look death in the face and live two-faced toward the future: live each day as if it were your last—as if it were complete in itself. At the same time, live each day as if it were your first—as if it were the first step in a brand new journey, a fresh start in your "call" to make history.

> There are more things in heaven and earth, Horatio, than are dreamt of in your philosophy.
>
> —*HAMLET*, ACT 1, SCENE 5, LINE 166

3) To Reclaim the Narrative Meaning of "Good News"

There is also this third reason why the world needs the Christian metanarrative more today than ever before: the gospel essence of

Christianity is "good news." In cultures where there is no concept of "news," the *euagelion* is more effectively translated as "good stories." The language of story is the language of the gospels. And the "good stories" are not ideas about God but activities of God, especially God's act of smashing death's dominion through a rolled-away stone. Each of the four gospels generates "good stories" of God raising the dead, with each gospel writer using his own language and images and idiosyncrasies (John's "I am's," Matthew's "the kingdom of heaven is like's," Mark's duh-ciples, Luke's fetish for detail). But within the great diversity of imagery and language and styles of expression, the good stories all revolve around the same grand narrative. The shape of Scripture is narrative, not philosophy, and any metanarrative that is shaped by Scripture ought to take the shape of Scripture.

A friend of a friend is a dermatologist. His favorite definition of dermatology is the race to treat a problem before it goes away on its own. But my pick of my friend's friend's sayings is the one that states there are only two things you need to know about dermatology: "If it's dry, make it wet; if it's wet, make it dry."

Likewise, there are only two things you need to know about Christianity, as we know it today. Both things are found in the same six-word statement: Christianity is *not* what you think.

The modern-era metanarrative relied on reason, offering the world a Christian "belief system." It was all about creating the right worldview. Just as modernity aimed to eradicate the mysteries of the world and substitute the encyclopedic certainties of a new science called applied reason, so Christianity sought to reinvent itself as a rational faith and set out to conquer mystery. It came to look at the scientific method as the preferred framework for tracking the truths of God. Even if it wasn't possible to achieve complete certainty, or have everything bolted down, explained, and tidied up, mystery was at best unhelpful.

Show me where in the Bible Jesus desired, or designed, to construct a system of truth in rational forms rather than relational forms? For Jesus, truth is not a philosophy or a matter of thought. Truth is a matter of relationships and realities. Jesus didn't offer the world a new belief system. He offered the world a new heart—a new heart for God, a new heart for yourself, a new heart for truth, a new heart for life, a new heart for others. This is the divine story of relationships, a far cry from the rational or scientific proof of God. It is also a far cry from the way science, not religion, supplies the metaphors and the stories that currently shape our world and our sense of what it means to be human.

Jesus didn't lift up Plato or any other philosopher and say, "Of such is the kingdom of heaven." Jesus lifted up a child, some say it was most likely Peter's child. And if the apple doesn't fall far from the tree, it was a rebellious, impetuous, high-strung, and hyperactive but simple child. With this child serving as metaphor, Jesus said, "Of such is the kingdom." Jesus even warned, "Do not despise one of these little ones."[28]

The icon of Christianity is not a thinker sitting down with his head in his hand.[29] The Icon of Christianity is a Savior nailed to a cross with the world in his hands.

We are not just in the thinking business. Christianity is more a world of poet and storyteller than philosopher and scientist. Biblical scholar Thomas Schmidt calculates that "the ratio of poetry to pure doctrine in the Bible is at least fifty to one, and most of the rest— including the life and teachings of Jesus—consists of stories and parables."[30] Faith is present to us as much in the unsayable as in the spoken word. The Christian metanarrative does not lead to detached Enlightenment so much as to engaged Enchantment.

> There are only two ways to live your life.
> One is as though nothing is a miracle.
> The other is as though everything is a miracle.
>
> —ATTRIBUTED TO ALBERT EINSTEIN[31]

4) To Reflect the Totalizing Nature of the Gospel

Finally, we need the Christian metanarrative because the gospel itself is totalizing. Its truth claims are universal. Every movement needs a metanarrative to stay alive, but none more so than Christianity. Its DNA is such that if there is no compelling story around which to gather, we won't gather. The metanarrative is what makes a Christian run. For Christians to acquiesce in the belief that religion can no longer provide people with a coherent and compelling story of their world and their identity and role in the world is for Christianity to put on its death mask.

There is only one reason you should be a Christian. Because it's true. Not because it's good for you; not because you'll be healed if you believe it; not because it brings peace and goodwill into the world. The only reason you should be a Christian is because God is God and because Jesus is the Way, the Truth, and the Life.

> We are alive within mystery, by miracle.
>
> —WENDELL BERRY[32]

The defining characteristic of Christianity is the metanarrative of God reconciling the world to God through Christ. The Christian metanarrative is a metaperson: Jesus the Christ. Every knee must bend to the truth that God calls "all people everywhere"[33] into relationship. But every culture rightfully creates a Jesus in its own image. The story of the Scriptures is the grand story of who God is and what God is doing in the world through Jesus the Christ.

This begs the question: "So who is God, and what is God doing?" The Christian story of everything is the story of a loving God *who* "so loved the world"[34] that God is *doing* everything God can do to pursue a relationship with all that God made, a relationship that ushers us into the kingdom of God—the new heaven and new earth of a redeemed creation and a reformed humanity. Whether you are young, old, or middle-aged; Jewish, Muslim, or Christian;

African, Asian, or Anglo; the truth is universal: the "secret place of the Most High"[35] is now dwelling among us and within us. A loving God is ushering us into the ways and wisdom of the kingdom (*malkuth* in Hebrew, *basileia* in Greek).

In short, the Christian metanarrative is the story of God's kingdom.

3

THE PRESENCE
THAT DELIVERS LIFE

God's Narrative Is Deceptively Simple

Regnum Dei Deus est.
The kingdom of God is God.
—ORIGEN

J esus taught us to pray using these words: "Your kingdom come…"[1] This is God's grand narrative in just three words.

One of the very few things biblical scholars agree on is that the "kingdom of God" is the cornerstone of Jesus' preaching, teaching, and healing. The phrase never appears in the Hebrew Scriptures (except in Targumic form), but it became commonplace in first-century Judaism. Jesus took a contemporary catch phrase about

God's activity in the world and made it into the centerpiece of his ministry.[2] Jesus introduced into history the kingdom metanarrative.

So that's it? The metanarrative of "Your kingdom come" is all we need? Surely there has to be more than simply Jesus preaching "the good news of the kingdom of God."[3]

Why do such questions live so close to the surface, ready to discount or marginalize what Jesus so clearly set forth as primary?

"THY KINGDOM COME..."

There is something of the Gnostic inside every one of us. How else to explain the seduction of *The Da Vinci Code?*[4] We all yearn for secret, privileged knowledge and the elite status such gnosis confers. The novelist and semiotician Umberto Eco alerts us to this danger through the voice of the narrator in *Foucault's Pendulum:*

> Hadn't Agliè spoken of the yearning for mystery which
> stirred in the age of the Antonines? Yet someone had just
> arrived and declared himself the Son of God...made flesh,
> to redeem the sins of the world. Was that a run-of-the-
> mill mystery? And he promised salvation to all: you had
> only to love your neighbor. Was that a trivial secret?...
> And yet they, who now had salvation within their grasp...
> [those who yearned for mystery] turned deaf ears. Is that
> all there is to it? How trite.... The mystery of the Trinity?
> Too simple: there had to be more of it.[5]

This is the problem we encounter with the Christian metanarrative. The "secret" seems so simple, so trite. Is that all there is? Every day, just put the kingdom of God first "and all these things will be given to you as well"?[6] When you pray every day, just say, "Your kingdom come"?[7]

DECEPTIVE SIMPLICITY

There is nothing more simple than the Christian metanarrative of the kingdom of God. But this "secret" is deceptively simple. For its very simplicity masks a complex of contrarian and secretive right relationships that rule the kingdom of God.

We are not the only ones confused by Jesus' use of the kingdom metaphor. Some of his followers plotted to "take him by force to make him king."[8] Some still are trying to do that today. But The Presence spreads through the world, not under the heraldry of King Jesus, but through seeds and leaven that seldom carry labels of origin.

Jules Glanzer is the dean of George Fox Evangelical Seminary. During a conversation about the biblical understanding of the kingdom, Jules reported on some fascinating research he was conducting. He compared the verbs we usually use with the noun "kingdom," and the verbs the Scriptures use. The contrast is striking.

We use verbs like "build" the kingdom, or "bring in" the kingdom, or "advance" or "establish" the kingdom. Many books have been written on how to "achieve" the kingdom of God. But the verbs the Bible uses are very different. The kingdom is something we "enter" or "find" and then "cherish." The kingdom is "given"; it's a gift that is "received." We can live a "no fear" life because "it is your Father's good pleasure to give you the kingdom."[9]

In other words, the kingdom of God is not something we "build" or "promote" or "push forward." The kingdom is not something we "bring in," but something we "enter" and "receive." The kingdom is even something that "comes," and sometimes only comes "close,"[10] with the cells of our consciousness too weak to pick up its signals. It is good to know that "close" now counts in horseshoes, hand grenades, and holiness.

Christianity keeps stubbing its TOE on this mistaken understanding of the kingdom as something we achieve and accomplish rather than enter and join. The language of the kingdom has drawn around itself a whole tangle of theological and cultural attachments that has turned Christianity's "grand stories" into stereotypes that can be more heinous than luminous. That's why there is much fusing and confusing of the kingdom of God with the USAmerican Dream, or the gross national product, or a social agenda, or a political strategy of liberation. That's also why all too often the kingdom of God can get co-opted by the "kingdom of self,"[11] which is based on the self-fashioning and self-fulfillment of "looking out for number one."

There is an old saying from Bible 101 that is meant to draw a distinction between the focus of Jesus' preaching and the focus of the early church: "Jesus preached the kingdom of God; the church preached Jesus." The saying is true as far as it goes. If you look at the central message of Jesus, it was always the kingdom of God. If you look at the central message of the early church, it was always Christ crucified and raised from the dead.

But the saying doesn't go far enough. This alleged distinction between the kingdom preaching of Jesus and the Jesus preaching of the early church has injected bad blood into the veins of Christianity. Two warring camps have battled over the real meaning of the word *Christian*. The joy of one camp's desiring is justice—these are the ones whose focused commitment is on the kingdom preaching of Jesus. The joy of the other camp's desiring is Jesus—these are the ones whose focused commitment is on the Jesus preaching of the church. The history of the church is a sacred but scarred story because of this blood feud between social justice and evangelism, between the "social gospel" and the "personal gospel." And in recent years a third blood strain has emerged, whose object of desire is the sheer joy of desiring (but that's yet another story).

> [The Beatitudes] contain a message that would save the world. What a pity that Christians have been listening to the message for two thousand years, but they are like stones lying in the water for centuries, never soaking up a single drop.
>
> —GANDHI[12]

In spite of two thousand years of sword crossings and trench warfare over the meaning of *Christian*, the real significance of the word still sleeps until this distinction is addressed and resolved. We might even say that the real history of Christianity remains unwritten, because its history is awaiting the rebirth and reawakening of the word *Christian*. Instead of this being a "wintry season" for Christianity, I believe the twenty-first century is Christianity's springtime. Far from the paranoia that fuels the fear that the postmodern era is humming the death knell of Christianity, this is the reveille of new birth for Christian faith and practice. We are moving toward a Christianity that is more beautiful and fruitful than anything we have yet seen.

THE JESUS UNDERSTANDING OF KINGDOM

In one moment the distinction between the kingdom and Jesus collapsed forever. In the rending of the Temple curtain when Jesus was hanging on the cross, they both became the same. As Origen first trumpeted to deaf ears, Jesus *is* the kingdom. In the presence of Jesus is found the presence of the kingdom. Just as in Jewish doctrine, the Torah didn't so much come from heaven as the Torah is itself heaven.[13] In the same way in Christian doctrine, Jesus is himself the kingdom. Just as Jesus is the One who Is, who Was, and who Is to Come, so the kingdom has come, is coming, and is now here. The kingdom of God *is* the presence of Jesus. "Lo, I am with you always…"[14]

That is why I propose we use another name for the kingdom of God. Instead of "kingdom" language, what if we were to approach the

Christian metanarrative as "The Presence." Christianity's Big TOE is not a Theory of Everything but a Truth of Everything: The immediate presence of the kingdom is found in Jesus. Jesus *is* the Truth of Everything. When Jesus said, "I am the way, and the truth, and the life," he immediately followed it with "no one comes to the Father but through *Me*."[15] Notice he did not say through "us," but through "me." Christ is both passport and port of entry to The Presence.

When Jesus preached the kingdom of God, he was showing us how The Presence is among us, around us, and in us. Jesus wants to live his resurrected life among us, and around us, and in us. To talk about "accepting Jesus into your heart" or "letting God into your life" is problematic for precisely this reason. Your heart is a pretty small package to stuff Jesus into. We are being called to become part of the body of Christ and to join in Jesus' ongoing ministry in the world. God wants *us* to join the divine life, to join in what God is doing in the world, to become part of God's life, to participate in the Godlife relationship. The promise of the gospel is not only that we can "practice The Presence," but we can join in The Presence and become The Presence. Together, we are the body of Christ. And in and through his body, the church, Christ is physically present in the world. The grand stories of Christianity are the ways in which we become Christ's "presences" in the world today.

The kingdom of God is The Presence of God in the world. "The kingdom of God is not coming with things that can be observed; nor will they say, 'Look, here it is!' or 'There it is!' For, in fact, the kingdom of God is *among* you."[16] Some translations say "within" or "inside" you. We are invited to enter The Presence, to receive the gift of Presence, to live in The Presence and let The Presence live in us. We grow as disciples by spending time in The Presence and by The Presence's spending time in us.

The Presence comes to go. We don't "build" it or "bring it in." We receive The Presence as a gift. That is why, when heaven is mentioned in the gospels, the word refers more often to how you live now than what happens when you die. Heaven means that we are ushered into The Presence. Hell means ultimately to be shut off from The Presence.[17]

The kingdom as The Presence is not a new insight that was introduced by Jesus. "It is not in heaven.... Neither is it beyond the sea.... [It] is very near to you; it is in your mouth and in your heart for you to observe."[18] The psalmist could think of nothing better than to "sit down in the High God's presence."[19]

Earlier names for The Presence include:
- Shalom (practicing the presence of peace)
- Shekhinah (allowing The Presence to dwell within us)
- Selah (pausing in praise and hanging in this moment of Presence)
- Hosanna (celebrating The Presence)
- Shabbat (sabbathing The Presence)
- Schema (discerning the voice of The Presence)
- Torah (living The Presence)

But with Jesus came the fullness of The Presence, not just "fullness of joy"[20] but "fullness of life." It is one thing to talk about a "relationship with Jesus" and understand it propositionally. To understand it relationally, you enter a whole new world of Presence living and dying. "Think not thou canst sigh a sigh," wrote William Blake about The Presence, "and thy maker is not by."[21]

Still, there is one reason why I resisted for so long using the language of "The Presence." It is too closely associated with Brother Lawrence's *Practice of the Presence of God*, a book that has become one of the prime classics of Western spirituality. Nicholas Herman was a French army officer who was severely wounded during the Thirty Years' War. At age forty-five he entered the religious community of the Carmelites in Paris (the same order as Saint Teresa of Avila), where he became a lay brother famous for his integration of work and worship—his lifetime kitchen "work" of washing dirty pots and pans and his monastic "worship" of God. His conversations and letters were collected after his death and published with the title *The Practice of the Presence of God*. Brother Lawrence was known for his unceasing meditation on the Trinity and his ability to entertain the highest of thoughts in the lowliest of places. Brother Lawrence modeled the possibility of cultivating a life of contemplation no matter where you are or what you do.

I love Brother Lawrence's spirit, especially his demonstration of how the repeated practice of spiritual acts can become habits and even second nature. Brother Lawrence's spiritual classic has inspired numerous Christians, both Catholic (see the letters of the seventeenth-century French bishop François Fénelon) and Protestant (see Joel S. Goldsmith's spirituality classic, *Practicing the Presence*).[22] But the phrase "practice of the presence" has become a code for talking about a life of meditation and contemplation. More recently, books on practicing the presence have become another way of talking about how to put into practice "the principles of spiritual living."[23]

A life of thinking about God, or a life of putting into practice certain spiritual principles or living out of a certain Christian worldview, is not what I mean by practicing The Presence. The Presence is more about communion than contemplation. The Presence is the love of God active in our world. Paul talked about how we are "always carrying in the body the death of Jesus, so that the life of Jesus may also be made visible in our bodies."[24] When Jesus is made visible, the kingdom comes. When "thy kingdom comes," The Presence is made present.

It is no longer just the Word that we hold in our hearts. It is now the "Living Word" made The Presence.

THE PRESENCE THAT ABIDES

One of the most frequently used biblical words for how the Word interacts in our lives is "abide." Jesus said, "If you abide in me, and my words abide in you, ask for whatever you wish, and it will be done for you."[25] The book of 1 Peter promises that the Word of God forever "lives and abides" among those who are born from above.[26] The book of 1 John testifies to the power that comes when "the word of God abides in you."[27]

But what does it mean for the Word to abide in us? The Greek meaning of the English word *abides* is a relational word. It means "make home with" or to "remain in relationship with." When you're abiding in the Word, you become swept up into The Living Presence where "rightness" pervades every relationship—with God, with others, and with creation.

Why do we have church? To "abide" in The Presence. To be sure, not many (if any) Christians would give that as an answer to the question, "Why do we have church?" Answer: "To abide in *The Presence*."

But in worship what are we really doing? We are flushing out that which is keeping us from abiding in The Presence, as we flesh out those things that keep us abiding in The Presence. Church is not here for us. We are here for the church, and the church is here for the world. The church is not a provider of religious goods and services. The church is a covenant community of people who together abide in The Presence. Worship is not all about the hour we're together. Worship is all about the week we've been apart, and the week we're about to enter. Christianity is not a Sunday experience, a one-hour Sunday spectacular. We have made worship the whole of religion, whereas in truth the purpose of worship is to usher each other "in," and more importantly, to usher each other "out," so that we will continue to abide in The Presence.

The kind of Presence we are called to practice in our world is the same Presence Jesus practiced. The Presence comprises the six most multilayered monosyllabic words in the English language: "For God so loved the world." Indeed, the essence of the Christian metanarrative of The Presence can be distilled into just three monosyllabic words: "I love you."

How to Say "I Love You" in Twenty Languages

Arabic: *Ana Behibak/Behibek*

Burmese: *Chit Pa De*

Dutch: *Ik Hou Van Jou*

English: I Love You

French: *Je T'aime*

German: *Ich Liebe Dich*

Greek: *S'Agapo*

Hindi: *Mai Tumse Pyar Karta Hoo*

Italian: *Ti Amo*

Japanese: *Kimi O Ai Shiteru*

Lingala: *Nalingi Yo*

Mandarin Chinese: *Wo Ai Ni*

Navaho: *Ayor Anosh'ni*

Norwegian: *Eg Elskar Deg*

Polish: *Kocham Cie*

Russian: *Ya Tebia Liubliu*

Spanish: *Te Amo*

Swedish: *Jag Älskar Dig*

Welsh: *'Rwy'n Dy Garu Di*

Zulu: *Ngiyakuthanda*[28]

The Presence in the Three Hardest Words

In these three words is the essence of The Presence: "I love you." In these three words is the essence of a biblical lifestyle: "I love you."

Of course, Christians are many things. Christians are people who love beauty and truth and goodness; people who welcome strangers, confront danger with a light heart, and who, in the face of death, choose life. They are people who, in the face of violence and hatred, choose hope. And they are much more.

But above and beyond everything else, Christians are people whose presence speaks the three words of The Presence: "I love you." The problem is that these three monosyllabic sounds are the three hardest words in the English language to get right. We live in a culture where the "I" has become a god, where "love" is far from being another name for Christ, and where people choke on the word "you" (if they can manage to say it at all).

In the pages that remain, we'll look at these three simple words and how the Christian metanarrative offers people a new identity ("I"), a new integrity ("love"), and a new intimacy ("you").

That is, if we can learn to say them right.

PART II

THE "I LOVE YOU" STORY

4

"I"

Receiving a New Identity

Put on the new self, created to be like God.
—Ephesians 4:24, TNIV

O h, the power and pride of the perpendicular: "I."

Notice how we always capitalize our I's.

Notice how the letter "I" even looks like the Tower of Babel: a steel dagger stabbing the heavens and saying, "Look at me! Look what *I* can do!"

But beware: Pride doesn't come before a fall. Pride *is* the Fall. Sin is the gravitational collapse of the I—the black-hole tendency of particularly large egos to fall in upon themselves. There is nothing so dark as the darkness within the I. The enormity of evil lurks in the perpendiculars of the I.

No matter how problematic this rod of egoistic steel is, however, we can't simply ignore the I, since we will never get "I love you" right if we don't first get "I" right. Without a Jesus understanding of who we are as individuals, we will never be capable of approaching the Jesus practice of love and of loving others.

GODIFYING THE I

The first-person pronoun "I" is the most godified word in the English language.

It was said that the late actor Marlon Brando's two favorite words were *Marlon* and *Brando*. The same could be said of you and me; simply insert your name or mine in the end of the previous sentence. *Tonight Show* pioneer Jack Paar once commented on humorist Steve Allen: "I'm fond of him—but not as much as he is."[1] The great Russian writer Maxim Gorky once suggested that there could be no room for God and novelist Leo Tolstoy in one universe. Ousted Iraqi dictator Saddam Hussein selected Frank Sinatra's version of "My Way" as the theme song for his fifty-fourth birthday.

In spite of all its protestations to the contrary, postmodern culture is more addicted to the Sinatra Doctrine ("I did it *my way*") than to the Streisand Doctrine ("People who need people").

One of my favorite writers' stories involves two authors who were talking at a party. One went on and on about all the great reviews his most recent book had received. Then checking himself, he said to the other author, "Well, enough about me. Let's talk about you. What do *you* think about my latest book?"

I think about that story when I find myself in certain emerging-church circles, where the I by itself is a *persona non grata*. It's all about community, and any I assertiveness is pounced on and put in its place. But when you read what both the emerging and the inherited church are blogging about, you learn far more about the writer's own life and state of mind than you do about God or Christian community. And even when Christians are writing about community, the subject has no center other than themselves.[2] It is the self, not God, that is at the core of contemporary spirituality.

DEMONIZING THE I

The first-person pronoun "I" is the most demonized word in the English language.

An old story tells about the ascent into heaven of a great spiritual teacher who knocked at the gates of paradise for admission. After some time, God came to the door and inquired, "Who is there? Who knocks?"

"It is I," came the confident response.

"Sorry, very sorry. There is no room in heaven. Go away. You will have to come back some other time."

The good man, surprised at the rebuff, went away puzzled. After several years, which he spent in meditation and pondering over this strange reception, the man returned and knocked again at the gate. He was met with the same question and gave a similar response. Once again he was told that there was no room in heaven; it was completely filled at that time. Try again later.

In the years that passed, the teacher soaked his soul deeper and deeper in the Scriptures, pondering in his heart the truth of life. After a long period of time had elapsed, he knocked at the gates of heaven for the third time.

Again God asked, "Who is there?"

This time the man's answer was, "Thou art."

The gates opened wide as God said, "Come in. There never was room for Me and thee."[3]

The I is becoming increasingly problematic, with some segments of science suggesting not just that there is no God, but that there is no I—that we are nothing but a series of chemical reactions, not a soul or a spirit, and that consciousness is a secondary result of chemical processes in the brain. We are not personalities or even persons, but simply accumulations of atoms and some random chemical reactions.

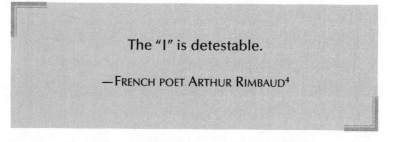

The "I" is detestable.

—FRENCH POET ARTHUR RIMBAUD[4]

Every totalitarian impulse in history has attempted to crush the I out of existence. One philosopher, concerned about incipient fascism in the postmodern, calls for "community," has named "The Dangerous Pronoun" not as "I" but "We."[5] The historical perspective tends to bear him out. In fact, the identity marker of a totalitarian age is the subjection of the individual to the community: it is 1944, at the height of the Holocaust in which six million Jews will die, yet Austrian philosopher Ludwig Wittgenstein (a man of Jewish descent) warns of getting lost in the numbers: "No cry of torment can be greater than the cry of one man." Or again (in another translation): "*No* torment can be greater than what a single human being may suffer." One more try: "The whole planet can suffer no greater torment than a *single* soul."[6]

When the individual exists for the sake of society, that's fascism.

I picked up on eBay a 5 Reichmark coined during the Third Reich. On one side is an image of Potsdam Church, above which is the swastika. Stamped on the edge in German are these words: "Public Interest Comes Before Self Interest." Similarly, Marxian thought derided individual rights as an ideological mask for the protection of existing structures of domination. The communist revolution in China and its imposition of "Mao suits" as the national uniform was an attempt to make everyone look and think the same. Fittingly, it was the twentieth-century's fight against totalitarian regimes that launched the tradition of marked individual graves for soldiers who died in battle.[7]

What's in It for Me?

Postmoderns have a *huge* "What's in it for me?" button. And they're always pushing it. The sovereignty of the self now reigns supreme. This whole culture encourages people to get drugged on the fumes of their egos. The big panacea of our time: "Just love yourself a little more."

If you think I'm exaggerating, take this test, which was first proposed by the Spanish philosopher Miguel de Unamuno. He posed the following choice for every person: you can create amazing works of art that would last forever, but only anonymously; or you can have your name live on in legend, even though your works would be totally forgotten. Which would you pick to survive: anonymous beauty or a legendary, famous name?

The "been there, done that" mentality is another expression of our ego addiction. Gregory H. Hemingway wrote a biography of his father, Ernest Hemingway, titled *Papa*. In 1976 he wrote these haunting words about his father's various divorces while serving the muse of "I":

> He would feel himself beginning to stagnate after he had
> been married to one wife for a while [but]…the periodic
> injection of high-octane creative energy left more of a
> hangover of contrition and remorse each time…. It takes
> something out of you to look back at your wife and your
> children by the side of the road and see that dazed look
> on their faces.[8]

As long as the I has not been de-idolized, marriage becomes a holding pen, a way station until something better comes along or the needs of the I change. If not "fully satisfied," the I can make a hasty exit or an exchange, upgrading to a more up-to-date model. It is commonly thought that life should come with such a satisfied-customer guarantee.

There is a big difference between the I curving in on itself and the I digging deeper within itself. The more the I gets curved, the more it becomes god, and the more isolated and lonely it gets, throttled by its parochial pities and dreams.[9] Management guru Ken Blanchard names "ego" as an acronym for "edging God out."[10] Ego is the most voracious carnivore that eats away the soul.

When are you *least* Christian? When your I is fat and curvy. When "it's all about me." When are you *most* Christian? When your I is straight and narrow. When your world revolves around God, others, and creation.

I will never forget sitting next to a woman on a flight out of Houston. From the puffing of her face and the bruised, black-and-blue sections of her complexion, I could tell she was on her way home from cosmetic surgery. I had just been reading about the popularity of extreme makeovers, even plastic surgery being done on hands to make them look younger. The year before this (2003), two million women in the US got Botox treatments. That's just women. That's just in the US. No one wants to talk about the finding by the American Society of Plastic and Reconstructive Surgeons that more people die annually as a result of liposuction procedures than from breast cancer, motor accidents, or homicide.[11]

After my seatmate pulled tight her seatbelt, she took a book from her Prada bag and began to write in it. The book, published in a journal format, was titled *All About Me*.[12]

We even talk about ourselves and call it prayer. Listen to some of our "all about me" prayers:

- Lord, help me out today.

- Lord, strengthen my body and give it endurance.
- Lord, give me the wisdom to face this challenge.

Compare the amount of time we spend asking God to help us pursue our goals and purposes with the time we spend inhabiting The Presence and sonogramming The Presence to discern how we can pursue God's purposes, how our life can fit into God's dreams.[13] British preacher Austin Farrer describes a lot of our prayers like this:

> Suppose a musical composer were conducting his own newly written symphony; and suppose the little man who does the drums were suddenly to put up his hand, and ask to have the score altered—he hadn't a sufficiently interesting part. What could the composer do, but explain to him the structure of the piece? And what answer can our prayers or wishes discover, other

In every authentic religious experience, the most characteristic expression is prayer. Because of the human spirit's constitutive openness to God's action urging it to self-transcendence, we can hold that every authentic prayer is called forth by the Holy Spirit.

—POPE JOHN PAUL II[15]

than this—to be told to study the way the world goes, and why?[14]

I'm not suggesting that we should abandon intercessory prayer. In fact, God has so structured the universe that our participation can actually shape the outcome of history as well as the outcome of each day. My favorite prayer of petition is one for which I've lost the source; it has become such a part of my life. (Apparently, I'm not the only one, since there are 1.6 million hits of it on the Internet.)

> Dear God, so far today I've done all right. I haven't gossiped. I haven't lost my temper. I haven't been greedy or grumpy or nasty or selfish. In fact, I haven't done anything wrong at all.
>
> I'm really pleased about all that but, God, in just a few minutes I'll be getting out of bed and, from then on, I'll be needing lots of help. Amen.[16]

Popular essayist and novelist Anne Lamott begins every day with two words spoken over and over again: "Help me, help me, help me."[17] Every one of us needs all the help we can get. Still, the model morning prayer would be one that is focused not on the self, but on The Presence. And it is a prayer that would not end without lifting up one-third of the world's people who live on less than two dollars per day, and the one in four who live on less than one dollar per day. Shouldn't prayer be less about the glory of the self and more about the glory of God? Shouldn't our prayers be less about the I as God's address and more about God's addresses in the world?

THE VALUE OF I

For all its potential for abuse, misuse, and God-denying self-obsession, we still can't simply obliterate the I as if we're just not that important. Nor can we pretend that the world could function quite nicely without us. The I is essential.

In point of fact, the I is the duct tape of Christianity. It may not be pretty or elegant, but the I begins every "I love you." It's not a random afterthought, not a disposable subject, not a polite obligatory mention. Love *begins* with I.

The I may have been defined differently in the past, but it was always there. Those of us within the Protestant tradition owe much to Martin Luther's "Here I stand." Yet the blatant egotism of the reformer's first-person singular stance is inescapable. One monk standing alone, picking a fight with the whole of the church's teaching authority? That's I writ big.

"Every man is obliged to say," observed the rabbis, "for my sake the world was created."[18] One of my spiritual disciplines is to laboriously read every name in the Bible's many torture lists of begats. Each list of names is a protest against all totalitarian attempts to efface individuality. There are no undocumented aliens in God's economy. We are strangers on earth, to be sure. But God knows the name of each one of us.[19]

No individual is expendable. Inasmuch as it can be said that God "needs" any person, God needs *every* person. In the famous words of the Mishnah (Sanhedrin 4:5), the human race is descended from one couple, Adam and Eve, reminding us that to destroy a single life is to destroy a whole world, and whoever saves a single life saves a whole world.[20]

Up until the Enlightenment, the world was structured in such a way that people literally inherited a "self." Your accident of birth fixed your fate for life. The I was defined by one's family, one's tribe, one's socioeconomic standing. The notion that the I is a free, autonomous, vacuum-sealed, nuclear self that covers a core identity to be discovered and explored apart from nature, community, and God was virtually nonexistent. What "identity issues" existed were those of making peace with, and making the best of, one's predetermined lot in life.

> "Individualization" consists in transforming human "identity" from a given into a "task"…needing to become what one is is the hallmark of modern living.
>
> —SOCIOLOGIST ZYGMUNT BAUMAN[21]

Not so today. We live in a world of unprecedented freedom to choose and control our lives. The "identity issues" of the I today are not ones of making peace with the self one inherited, or making the best of things, but making a very self in the first place. Today we invent ourselves, seeking to manufacture who we are apart from community, family, environment, society, and God. The notion that individuals should and do control their own lives is a modern Western idea. We have been on a quick historical journey from what scholars have called the "self-made man" to the "man-made self."[22]

The sovereignty of I has only been exacerbated by consumer sovereignty. Once again, our arrival at this place has been a quick trip. The emergence of the consumer as a self-conscious historical agent possessing "rights" and needing "protection" didn't emerge on the scene until the nineteenth century.[23]

All this has brought us to where we are today: the search for truth has been replaced with the search for self. For the first time in history, the I can author itself, writing its own life story. It is no wonder that people are desperate to find do-it-yourself assembly kits for constructing a self, and the sales of self-help, self-esteem, how-to-be-a-success books testify to the amount of experimentation going on in the attempt to write on our own terms a personal, customized micronarrative.[24]

> In the future, everyone will be
> ordinary for fifteen minutes.
>
> —IRISH-AMERICAN NOVELIST MICHAEL COLLINS[25]

THE REAL IDENTITY ISSUE

The irony is that the more we are "on our own" in creating an identity, the more one of two things happens. Either we slowly lose our
carefully crafted identity, or we end up looking and sounding and
being just like everyone else. In both cases, we have no real identity.

Losing Your Identity

Identity theft is a reality—both physically and spiritually. Our I
rapidly becomes diluted and dispersed—even stolen. One in five of
us has been hit by the crime of identity theft, in which an imposter
obtains key pieces of information, such as Social Security and driver's
license numbers, and then uses the data for his or her own gain. To
twenty-first century burglars, the television and DVD player are far
less valuable than personal information they can steal from bank
statements and other documents.[26]

Our spiritual identity is stolen in a similar way. Does Scripture
not teach that the Evil One comes like a thief in the night to steal,
pillage, and plunder our identities as sons and daughters of God? In
fact, a key indicator of spiritual identity theft in postmodern culture
is the prevalence of the psychiatric diagnosis of "borderline personality disorder," which covers a multitude of symptoms that have one
thing in common: people are in desperate straits trying to compose
a coherent and compelling narrative for "who am I?" There are so
many choices and options that one's identity gets scattered and
fragmented.[27] Borderline personality disorder and its surging cousin,

multiple personality disorder, are psychological signposts of post-modern culture. My story isn't working for me, so I'll just try another. But I don't want to totally let go of the one that isn't working, so I'll simply add on other one.

The whole of "celebrity culture" can be seen as a narrative vehicle for people who are looking for a rewrite or a copyeditor (internal or external) to give them a bigger and better story line. From the standpoint of the celebrity, however, it's a Faustian deal, not with the devil but with vampires. The price of becoming a celebrity is the loss of self. Your very "self" is sucked out of you as you become a public possession. The notion of a "self" disappears since everything about you—your authenticity, integrity, selfhood—becomes a transaction with the public.

> Jesus is the copy editor of human life.
>
> —MEXICAN NOVELIST CARLOS FUENTES[28]

Gaining a Nonidentity

The second thing that often happens when we create our own I is this: everyone's I ends up looking alike. Personal identity becomes a nonidentity, a dog-tag identity of name, serial number, and brand logos that transmit the current cultural mores and beliefs on race, class, gender, and politics. We find out that we do not think so much as we are thought; we do not speak so much as we are spoken. And contrary to our conviction that we are free to create our own story, we find that the authority figure doing the thinking and speaking for us is most often the identity-creating community of pop culture.

In thinking we can create ourselves from scratch through choices and accepting or rejecting certain of the available alternatives, we are in fact being manufactured by a consumer culture in which sellers compete for our allegiance, and in exchange present us with a brand identity. The self-created I is in reality a prefabricated identity that comes off one assembly line or another (media culture, the self-esteem industry, and so forth).[29]

> Do you not know who you are?
>
> —APOSTLE PAUL[30]

THE PARADOX OF THE I

Are we truly free to "create ourselves"? Can we dress the bare bones of our life with narrative? Can we write and control our own story?

Well, yes and no.

Yes, We Can

We can write our own story because the autonomy of the I is like Mount Everest: it's not going anywhere. The possibilities of personhood are here to stay. In fact, God created us with free will, and while such personal autonomy is clearly open to abuse, it also is a gift from the empyrean heights. We can't dismiss our freedom to make choices as evil narcissism from the fiery pit of hell.

The real question is, How are we going to deal with Mount Me? Along with the freedom to create an I comes the responsibility for the I we create.[31] Without taking full and active responsibility for the I we are, and are becoming, we cannot possibly make the necessary commitments to abiding in The Presence and to living out "I love you."

> The final responsibility for each life is always the responsibility of the person whose life it is.
>
> —PHILOSOPHER KWAME ANTHONY APPIAH[32]

That is the qualified yes to the question on our ability to create an I by writing our own story. But notice that the yes of free will and self-creation is of necessity only a partial answer.

No, We Can't

The full answer to the question of the self-created I is also no, because the defining quality of the Christian life is living in The Presence. That means it's not true that every choice is all up to us. We are not totally free to create ourselves; we are free to accept an identity that has been chosen for us by The Presence. Every self-created edition of I is guilty of sedition.

The pronoun "I" is a paradox. Not only do the ends of I never meet, but the ends are headed in two opposite directions at the same time—upward and downward.[33]

In The Presence, we are given a new identity. That identity is comprised of two poles. For a full spiritual life, you need both affirmation and negation. Paul put it best: "I live; yet not I, but Christ liveth in me."[34] In the celestial calculus of The Presence, two is really one, and one is really two.

AFFIRMATION: "I LIVE..."

In the Grail legend, each knight began his search for the Holy Grail (the chalice of the blood of Christ) by entering the forest at a point where it was darkest and there was no path. And each did so alone.

Everyone enters the labyrinth of life alone.

Everyone enters the valley of the shadow alone.

Everyone passes through the gates of eternity alone.

Everyone stands before the Judgment Seat alone.

As surely as this book will reach its last page, your life will end. Your I will look death in the face with no one there but you and God. And what does that say about the current emphasis on community?

> I have called you by name, you are mine.
>
> —ISAIAH 43:1

Unlike a lot of the literature currently being written, where "community" is the new golden calf, Jesus does not let the community be the be-all and end-all. He elevates the individual in significant and telling ways. Even the sparrows that fly eventually fall, Jesus said. But every sparrow's fall does not go without the Father's notice. How much more, Jesus said, does the Father's love shadow each one of you?[35]

In fact, Jesus refused to let the community define either himself or his disciples. Jesus expected his disciples to define themselves in terms larger than their family and community defined them ("who are my mother and my brothers?").[36] They weren't to ask permission of their family before following Jesus ("No one who puts a hand to the plow and looks back is fit for the kingdom of God").[37] They were told not to let the traditions and expectations of the community determine their actions ("Let the dead bury their own dead").[38] To those who said, "Put family first," Jesus said, "I have come to set a man against his father, and a daughter against her mother."[39] To those who said, "Put tradition first," Jesus said, "I came to bring fire to the earth, and how I wish it were already kindled!"[40] Unless you are prepared to separate yourself from the community—from family, tradition, and even your very life—you can't carry the cross.

To be born into the world, and to walk into the unknown, we have to risk separating ourselves from others. Jesus turned his back on family and friends and established his identity in light of The Presence. The result was a strong sense of self that was "self-ish" (secure of self) but not "selfish" (full of self).[41] A strong sense of self and a strong sense of community are not mutually exclusive.[42]

Human beings set themselves apart from the animal kingdom by revealing the I in their faces. Humans are unique in the animal kingdom—there are *no* exceptions—in that humans make love face to face. And that face, with its mouth that smiles, its skin that blushes, its eyes that twinkle, is a window to the inimitable soul that grows within.

Our absorption into The Presence (our "oneness" with Christ) is not the oneness of Buddhism, where one's separate consciousness and I are lost in one's absorption into the universe. Rather, our absorption into The Presence completes our own personhood. Here is Richard Foster paraphrasing John Dalrymple:

> Union with God does not mean the loss of our individuality. Far from causing any loss of identity, union brings about full personhood. We become all that God created

us to be. Contemplatives sometimes speak of their union with God by the analogy of a log in a fire: "the glowing log is so united with the fire that it *is* fire," while, at the same time, it remains wood. Others use the comparison of a white-hot iron in a furnace: "Our personalities are transformed, not lost in the furnace of God's love."[43]

[What is a self?] Every moment that a self exists, it is in the process of becoming, for the self κατα δύναμιν [in potentiality] does not actually exist, is simply that which ought to come into existence.

—SØREN KIERKEGAARD[44]

NEGATION: "YET NOT I, BUT CHRIST LIVES WITHIN ME"

Our first act of autonomy is to limit our autonomy. To come to ourselves, we first need to get over ourselves. One of the greatest-ever spiritual insights was this notion that to gain life, to live, we must throw ourselves away. This is "the first law of spiritual dynamics," according to British sociologist David Martin: "Losing your life to find it."[45]

The goal of the Christian life is to lose oneself and use oneself up in a cause and creed, not of one's own making, but of God's own choosing. A love that does not insist on its own way or its own say is perhaps the greatest flash point of friction between the gospel and contemporary culture—between the Christian metanarrative and our own mininarratives. Even psychology and psychoanalysis have degenerated from a "study of the soul" (*psyche* is the Greek word for "soul") into a cult of self-help and self-esteem, which Frank Furedi aptly calls "a cultural myth for our times." Nicholas Emler calls it the "psychotherapeutic equivalent of snake oil."[46]

Whereas in the past a person said, "I am troubled," today he says, "I've got a problem,"[47] meaning that he has caught some malady or disorder, with new syndromes and disorders being discovered all the time.[48] Postmodern culture is filled with people who are less in love with their true selves than with their neuroses, and who are faithfully devoted to taking their pulse, monitoring their phobias, and medicating their ailments.[49] Our "issues" and "conflicted feelings" supposedly stem mostly from a failure to put ourselves first, a lack of self-esteem (even though studies of "high self-esteem" kids reveal that "confident children…are more likely to be racists, to bully others and to engage in drunk driving").[50] One loses track of the times the phrase "lack of self-esteem" is hauled out to perform its therapeutic task.

Ironically, as the church has sold itself out to a culture of self-absorption and consumption—presenting the gospel as a benefits package—there are approaches in consumer culture that reveal an understanding of the power of "losing oneself." The "losing oneself" shopping experience is built around "the Gruen transfer," named after the Los Angeles-based architect Victor Gruen, who gave us the

> Most of us want success and so achieve nothing.
> Jesus made himself nothing and so achieved
> abiding success. Most of us suppress our past
> and so pretend a future. Jesus was prepared
> to sacrifice his future to give us hope for our past.
> Most of us are tempted to use people and
> lose all respect. Jesus won respect by being
> willing to let others make use of him.
>
> —ALISON ELLIOT, THE FIRST WOMAN ELECTED MODERATOR
> OF THE CHURCH OF SCOTLAND'S GENERAL ASSEMBLY[51]

first design of a new breed of mazelike malls. The Southdale Mall (1954–1955) outside Minneapolis was designed in such a way that it delivered a key moment in the shopping-mall experience—the point where you "get lost" in shopping. You forget what you came to the mall to buy and submit to a barrage of shopping appeals.

But the point of "getting lost" in the shopping maze is still self-indulgence, not community betterment. The antidote to self-obsession and "therapism" is not "Algerism"[52] but altruism, not self-reliance but self-transcendence. Christian spirituality is a self-transcending experience of God through Christ by the gift of the Holy Spirit.[53] Rituals, the arts, retreats (I prefer to call them "advances"), spiritual disciplines—these are not means of discovering the self but of transcending the self.[54] The Christian metanarrative seeks self-transcendence, not self-fulfillment. Rather than seeking fulfillment, why aren't we seeking God?

We do have issues, but not the issues that readily come to mind:

- Our issue is not "What do I want?" but "What is wanted of me?"
- Our issue is not "How can you meet my needs?" but rather "How am I meeting the world's needs?"
- Our issue is not "What are my needs?" but "What is God needing of me?"
- Our issue is not "Am I on top?" but "Am I on tap?" Am I available for God to use?
- Our issue is not "How can I chart my own path?" but "How can I find and follow God's path?"
- Our issue is not "Take charge of your life" but "Let God take charge of your life."
- Our issue is not "See how special I am!" but "How Great Thou Art!"

Life is not "go Google yourself." Life is "go Google God." The I gets into trouble when it tries to be "like gods"—when the I pushes itself upward, not downward. The spiritual journey is one that starts with the baby cry of the self as the center of the universe but then avoids moving to the crybaby self as the center of the universe. Instead, it moves to the experience of others and of God. The course of biblical spirituality is away from the self. (What's not weird and perverse about the terrorists is the very thing that the culture thinks is weird and perverse: their willingness to die for their faith. What *is* weird and perverse about the terrorists is that they are willing to take innocent lives.)

Christianity is more self-sacrifice than self-fulfillment. "All we like sheep have gone astray; we have all turned to our own way."[55] Christianity holds out the truth that an ego trip is a journey to nowhere. It's a ticket to waywardness. In contrast, a spirituality of The Presence is another word for the collapse of egocentrism.[56] When we try to live by the standards of the USAmerican success story, we are living a lie. It's not a love story; it's a flawed and selfish story.[57] Whose measure of success will we adopt?

FILLING BY EMPTYING

Rick Pitino is the head basketball coach of the University of Louisville. His record of success in both the NCAA (at Providence College and with the Kentucky Wildcats) and the NBA (with the Boston Celtics and the New York Knicks) is legendary. Pitino's best-selling book *Success Is a Choice* outlines ten steps to success. Here's the "Pitino 10":

1. Build self-esteem.
2. Set demanding goals.
3. Always be positive.
4. Establish good habits.
5. Master the art of communication.
6. Learn from role models.

7. Thrive on pressure.

8. Be ferociously persistent.

9. Learn from adversity.

10. Survive success.[58]

Here's a completely different model of success: get over yourself; lay down the perpendicular. *Plerosis* ("filling") is found in *kenosis* ("emptying"). *Emptying* is the first word of the Christian love story.

Before the ritual we know as baptism, there were many cleansing rituals that were mandated of the devout Jew. One of these required the use of "cedar wood, and scarlet, and hyssop."[59] Each one of these ingredients was symbolically important to the rabbis. Cedar comes from the tallest of trees. Hyssop comes from the lowliest of bushes. The scarlet dye (Hebrew *tolaat*) comes from a worm. Since many of our physical and spiritual ailments come from pride (the lofty superiority of the cedar), healing only comes when we learn the humility of the hyssop and the abasement of the worm.[60] The "cedar, scarlet, and hyssop" is what led Jewish teachers to recommend that we think of every person we meet as our superior.[61]

The Presence says to our self-absorbed culture: You can't know "love" until you first lay down the perpendicular, until you first cross out the perpendicular, until you surrender and sacrifice the ego, until you keep your egos[62] under wraps. You can't be full of The Presence until you're empty of I. Pride is our greatest enemy, and humility is our greatest friend. To get the word "I" right, to be a "success" in The Presence, we first need to cross out the I. And when we cross it out, we make the I into a †, a cross that we take up as we follow the Christ in whom we live.

> All of us who rebel against the sovereign
> rule of God join in the rejection suffered by the Son,
> and the reconciliation he offers extends to all of us.
> Our part is to admit that we have exhausted our
> powers of self-direction (we've used all our
> ammunition, as it were) and submit finally to the
> rule and fellowship of God. We need to surrender.
> The atonement cannot easily be explained,
> but it can readily be experienced.
>
> —QUAKER SCHOLAR ARTHUR O. ROBERTS [63]

One of the greatest "success" stories of all time took place in Kentucky in the early twentieth century. Luther B. Bridgers served as a Methodist pastor. One winter evening in 1910 he was preaching at a revival meeting when he got word that he should return to his in-laws' home in Harrodsburg, Kentucky, as soon as possible. His wife and three sons were there, visiting her parents while he was conducting the revival.

By the time Bridgers got to Harrodsburg, all that was left of his in-laws' home, his wife, and his sons was ashes. He stood there, broken and heartbroken. In the flames of that one fire, he cried out, "All my life was wrecked…"

But then he went on:

All my life was wrecked by sin and strife,

Discord filled my life with pain,

Jesus swept across the broken strings,

Stirred the slumbering chords again.

And out of those ashes was born a song, "He Keeps Me Singing":

Though sometimes He leads thro' waters deep,

Trials fall across the way,

Tho' sometimes the path seems rough and steep,

See His footprints all the way.

(chorus)

Jesus, Jesus, Jesus,

Sweetest Name I know,

Fills my every longing,

Keeps me singing as I go.[64]

Success is trusting that wherever Christ leads, whether by still waters, into green pastures, or through the valley of the shadow of death, "surely goodness and mercy shall follow me,"[65] and all will be well.

OUR IDENTITY IN THE PRESENCE

The self can only be named and shaped in relation to The Presence. We are saved from ourselves so that we can look to Christ. Rather than looking in the mirror to seek our own face, the metanarrative of The Presence offers a life of seeking God's face.[66]

> One thing I ask from the LORD, this only do I seek: that I may dwell in the house of the LORD all the days of my life, to gaze on the beauty of the LORD and to seek him in his temple.... My heart says of you, "Seek his face!" Your face, LORD, I will seek. Do not hide your face from me.[67]

Gil Bailie is the founder and president of Cornerstone Forum. He believes we ought to learn from the early church fathers and talk more about the "person" than the "self."[68] And he defines the biblical understanding of "the person" in as radical a way as postmodern culture could imagine: "the one who does not come in his or her own name."

> The older I get, the more convinced
> I am that the space between
> communicating human beings
> can be hallowed ground.
>
> —MISTER ROGERS[69]

The word *person* was a throw-away term; it came from
persona, the mask of the Greek stage, and had no serious
philosophical significance until the church fathers used it
in trying to understand Jesus' great question, "Who do
you say that I am?" The church fathers realized that they
couldn't describe Christ as an entity all by himself. In the
Gospel of John he says, "Whoever has seen me has seen
the Father." He says: "I am in the Father and the Father
is in me." He says: "I do nothing on my own, but I say
only what the Father taught me."[70]

For Bailie, most powerful of all was Jesus' claim that "I came in
the name of my Father, but you do not accept me; yet if another
comes in his own name, you will accept him."

Nothing could be more contemporary than that. Anybody who doesn't come in his own name, we hold in
suspicion. The contemporary feeling is that you should
come in your own name, be your own person, toot your
own horn.[71]

Just as Jesus refused to be described except in relationship to the
One who sent him, so we need to always be establishing our identity
not in terms of who we are, but in terms of who Christ is. Our identity as a true self is found only as we latch on to Jesus with the full
force of our intellect, imagination, and emotions.

As tribal cultures experienced through their masked dances, a mask allows us to be free—able to feel and act in ways that we never would if our real face were showing. When we put on the persona of Christ, we are released to show our true colors.[72]

> Because God as love (and love as God)
> is an overflowing, an excess, an emptying,
> beyond its own limits, a letting go,
> life and discourse can be connective,
> celebrative, communicative.
>
> —JAMES H. OLTHUIS[73]

But our identity as an I needs also to be shaped in relationship to our dancing partners—to others who have chosen a similar identity and life-project of living in The Presence. I am who I am both because I have limited my autonomy so that I might receive the identity of Christ and because I am in relationship with a collective of identities who are on similar journeys. The I is more than a skin-wrapped ego. The true space of the I is not the space within or the space without but the space *between*, the space in the "midst," the space we share with others. Or as one scholar puts it, "The interplay of the individual and the interdependent yields a third entity: the connective self."[74] But then, isn't that what skin is? Connecting tissue that simultaneously gathers our various parts "in" and links the gathered whole "out" with the universe?

As we will see, the new identity we find in The Presence has meaning for each of us personally and also in community. And it realizes this double meaning through the agency of love—the second of the three hardest words.

5

"LOVE"

Receiving a New Integrity

> The important thing is not to think
> much but to love much.
>
> —SAINT TERESA OF AVILA

Noticing the dominance of the rain theme in the art and music of the Hopi people, an anthropologist asked a Hopi tribal leader why so many of his people's songs dealt with rain. The Hopi replied that it was because water is so scarce in the land where they live. He then asked the anthropologist: "Is that why so many of your songs are about love?"[1]

We live in a world that is awash in love songs and love stories but where love that looks beyond the I is as rare as windows and clocks in casinos. How are we to love and be loved? This is the hardest of questions being asked today. The verb form of "love" is missing in action. We stop with the first-person pronoun, I, and dismiss the crucial verb, love. How are we to love and be loved is the question the hip-hop group the Black Eyed Peas asked in their best-selling song: "Where Is the Love?"[2]

> ### make Love loved
>
> —SAINT THÉRÈSE OF LISIEUX'S LIFE MISSION STATEMENT[3]

NOT PURPLE RAIN

Love has almost become the spiritual equivalent of acid rain. The same modes of thought and action that create raindrops that literally devour cathedrals have likewise devoured our ability to love in the right meaning of the word—living for and lifting up what glorifies God. In the relationally polluted climate in which we live, love has a B-movie quality to it. We have "love interests" rather than "love covenants" or "love relationships." Teenagers either have given up on relationships (in favor of "hook-ups," "friends with benefits," "three-date rule," or "no-date rule") or are obsessed with soap-opera love and "celebrity" love. Trying to use the word "love" biblically in post-modern culture is like trying to steer your way safely through a chamber of horrors.

In our world of rampant "individualization" relationships are mixed blessings. They vacillate between a sweet dream and a nightmare, and there is no telling when one turns into the other. Most of the time the two avatars cohabit.

—SOCIOLOGIST ZYGMUNT BAUMAN[4]

A Jewish folk tale[5] demonstrates the confusion associated with the simple statement "I love you," while illustrating how difficult it can be to get the word "love" right:

> Once upon a time, an angler pulls a large pike out of the water. "Look at the size of this fish! I'll take it to the Baron. He loves pike."
>
> Hearing these words, the poor fish says to himself, "There's hope for me yet."
>
> When the fisherman presents himself at the gate of the manor house, the guard inquires: "What do you have?"
>
> "A pike for the Baron."
>
> "Great," replies the guard. "The Baron loves pike."
>
> Once again, the fish hears the words, and while he can hardly breathe as he is brought into the palace, he still finds hope: the Baron loves pike.

As he is brought into the kitchen, all the cooks get excited as they look at the fish, nodding to one another how much the Baron loves pike. The fish is then placed on a table, and the Baron himself enters and examines the fish. "Cut off the tail, cut off the head, and slit it this way."

With his last breath, the fish cries out in great despair, "Why did you lie? You don't love pike, you love yourself!"

The poor fish is as confused as we are by the different meanings of the same verb.

The most complex four-letter word in the English language? The most significant four-letter word in human history? The answer to both questions is the same: "love." Because it is so used, misused, and abused, "love" may well be the most unloved word in our language. More foolish things have been written about love than about any other word. Just think about the eight dumbest words ever written about love: "Love means never having to say you're sorry."[6]

The strangest thing ever said about love? Kierkegaard thought it

> Much is forgiven to them that love much.
>
> —PETER ABELARD'S FAVORITE QUOTE FROM THE BIBLE[7]

incredibly strange and "most stupid" that anyone would think of love existing "to a certain degree."[8] A person either loves with *all* or doesn't love at all.

The fifteen smartest words ever written about love? *Love God with all your heart, soul, strength and mind, and your neighbor as yourself.*[9]

The most beautiful love song ever written? It is not "Bridge Over Troubled Waters," as is commonly said. It is a song that sings of God's love affair with us: "God So Loved the World." Are we broadcasting this song on our life stations?

I once watched as a car emblazoned with fish symbols and other Christian logos pulled illegally into a handicapped parking spot. The driver hopped out and ran into Gold's Gym. Some Christians suffer, not just from a multiple personality disorder, but from a gross personality disorder. Why aren't Christians known as the greatest lovers in the world? The only county in the US that reports no people in any church congregation is Loving County, Texas. Could it be that if you're loving enough, you don't need churches?[10] Christians are not called to handle people with "kid gloves," but with love gloves.

The Presence not only gives us an identity for life; it provides an integrity to living that calls us back to reality after our repeated attempts to escape from reality. Love is The Presence living in us, the energy of God working in us. Salvation is basically the unleashing of the latent power of love in us. In this sense, salvation is not primarily about the afterlife or heaven, but about the integrity of our life on earth. Only love can undo on earth the depredations of the Fall.

Still, we can't say the word "love" right until we learn to say "I" right. Why? Because the true character of love is self-giving, the emptying and expending of oneself for the well-being of others. True love lays down the drawbridge of the I so that others can cross over into The Presence. "No one has greater love than this," Jesus said, than "to lay down one's life for one's friends."[11] You don't find love by looking for it; you find love by laying it down and letting it go.

> Christians are blissful people who can
> rejoice at heart and sing praises.
> Stamp and dance and leap for joy.
>
> —MARTIN LUTHER[12]

CUBIC INTEGRITY OF A "CIVILIZATION OF LOVE"

George MacLeod, founder of the Iona community, has a haunting meditation on the cleansing of the Temple:

> In the temple You threw out the money changers,
>   Lord Christ:
> down the steps and out of the door—
> and into the vacant aisles came the children
> shouting for joy and dancing round.

Here MacLeod contrasts the religious bureaucrats (I call them "ecclesiocrats") who follow the rules and pass resolutions and enforce regulations with the natural noises and exuberance of the children, oxygenating the Temple with the airy sounds of laughter and play.

> Too often we are the money changers:
> giving short change in spiritual things
> to many who seek the true coin:
> making the Church an institute
> when you want it to be a chaos of uncalculating love.[13]

What a definition of the church: "a chaos of uncalculating love"—a home for noisy children, creative artists, crazy people with absurd ambitions for peace and goodwill in our world.

> Drive out from our hearts
> our calculated offerings,
> our easy responses,
> and let child-like faith
> flood into us again.[14]

In his development of the metaphor of the church as the body of Christ, Paul encouraged the Ephesian Christians to think of themselves as a new temple, a temple of God.[15] It's no accident that on medieval maps Jerusalem is represented as the sacred heart of the whole world. The Temple was a symbol of The Presence, the divine presence in the midst of the people.[16] But with the death of Stephen, early Christians began to realize that a temple "made with hands" was no longer necessary, because an organic, living temple was present in the "body" of the church, and decentralized temples were present in the individual "living stones" that made up the church.

Paul then admits that the "love of Christ" defies description, but drawing from the Temple imagery he offers a multidimensional metaphor to help us know the unknowable: "I pray that you may have the power to comprehend, with all the saints, what is the breadth and length and height and depth, and to know the love of Christ that surpasses knowledge, so that you may be filled with all the fullness of God."[17]

In the Temple tradition extreme care was taken to get the dimensions exact, both in building measurements and furbishing the holy space. Aspects of heaven were duplicated in the Temple: darkness (Holy of Holies), veil of smoke, molten sea, and so forth. Architecture is theology that takes material form. In his letter to the Ephesian Christians, Paul invites us to think multidimensionally about the high art of the spiritual architecture of love, which fills us with the "fullness of God."[18]

Jesuit theologian Ignacio Ellacuría historicized a vision of the future that the Roman Catholic Church has long called a "civilization of love." Ellacuría contrasts it with the "civilization of wealth" and the "civilization of poverty" that dominate the world.[19] I beg your permission to adopt this powerful phrase, *civilization of love,* as the dream of The Presence, and to combine it with two of Paul's unique metaphors: the Temple imagery introduced to the Ephesians, and his exhortation to the Philippians that they "behave as a citizen"[20] of the kingdom of God and the gospel of Christ. Paul's claim

> By the witness of their dynamic and constructive power of love, Christians will thus lay the foundation of the "civilization of love."
>
> —POPE JOHN PAUL II[21]

to Roman citizenship, the greatest passport to influence and power in his day, was trumped by an even higher citizenship: he was a citizen of the kingdom of God. And citizenship in that civilization of love is built on a certain kind of gospel integrity, an integrity cubed by length and breadth and depth.

Whenever God gave construction projects to the people of Israel (the ark of Noah, ark of the covenant, the Temple in Jerusalem), the dimensions were specified down to the last cubit. A cubit was more than the eighteen or so inches comprising a man's forearm. A cubit was a shorthand way of describing the construction of a space that had multidimensionality.

This three-dimensional detailing of the lives of God's people appears everywhere in the Scriptures. The rabbis taught that "if two sit together, and words of the law pass between them, the divine presence abides between them."[22] When two people come together to study and learn, learning happens only when a third party, The Presence, enters into the process. When David said in the psalms, "I will walk with integrity of heart within my house," the word *tâm*, which we translate "integrity," really means "having it all together." To live with integrity, to live in The Presence, is to "have it all together."[23]

Jesus expanded that rabbinic saying, giving it new life, in his promise that "where two or three are gathered in my name, I am there among them."[24] Thus, the cubit measurement that was used to construct God's first building projects is replaced with a new, three-dimensional measurement for God's civilization of love. What makes the church the church? The Presence. There will never be just two when Christians gather. There will always be three. The risen Christ's final words reassure us: "I am with you always, to the end of the age."[25] As long as life is cubed, The Presence is present.

> It is only in the mysterious equations of love that any logic or reason can be found.
>
> —NOBEL LAUREATE JOHN NASH (A BEAUTIFUL MIND)[26]

THREE DIMENSIONS OF LOVE

The civilization of love is built on the following measurements:

- Love cubed by length: Love's temple knows no conditions—it knows only unconditional love and loyalty. Love's temple is totally open to God. There is no cap to the love of God, and there is no length to which the love of God won't go.

- Love cubed by breadth: Love's temple has no walls. A microcosm of creation, love's temple connects us to the mysteries of the cosmos, where stranger things than cherubim and seraphim abound.
- Love cubed by depth: In love's temple, the deeper you go the holier it gets. God's love reaches as far down as humans can go.

Every theological word falls short. Every religious word fails. When all words are said and done, only the word "love" remains. It's the word we say too easily, but not often enough.

Love Cubed by Length

The love that leads to golden anniversaries has integrity of length. And length is not simply the passage of time, marked in years and anniversary cards, but also the trouble loves goes to. You could think of it as long-suffering. It has to do with the lengths love goes to, the extent to which love extends itself. When you consider how far love will go, it doesn't make sense. Love is immoderate, intemperate, immediate. Love's conclusions are not arrivals but itineraries, not finished formulations but alluring possibilities and invitations.

In the modern world, we learned to say, "Come, let us reason together." Or in more philosophical words, "I think, therefore I am." But in the world that is being born, we must learn to say, "Come, let us love together." Or in more theological words, "I am loved, therefore I am."

Notice that the lifestyle of love—the life that is lived in The

Presence—is not based on "I love, therefore I am" but "I am loved, therefore I am."[27] Or in more biblically resonant words, "We love because he first loved us."[28] The difference is crucial. We are not self-empowering, autonomous individuals with a capacity to love. Our ability to love right is itself a gift, one that does not come from within but from a God who loves us in spite of our unloveliness. This gift from God makes us lovely and able to love like God loves.[29]

> Christian love is not softhearted exactly, but it does propose very decidedly not to let itself be entrapped and hardened in selfishness or hatred, and it has a very clear vocation to service.... Along with love comes hope. To be really new, the new human beings must be persons of hope and of joy in the building of a more just world.
>
> —THEOLOGIAN IGNACIO ELLACURÍA[30]

In his book *Agape and Eros,* Anders Nygren asserted that *agape* is a love that doesn't expect anything in return. But he was absolutely wrong.[31] There is no such thing as one-way love. And there is no such thing as self-less love. All love is relational. The notion that we can give love without receiving love violates the biblical understanding, where "Love is from God; everyone who loves is born of God and knows God. Whoever does not love does not know God, for God is love."[32] For us to experience love, we must receive the love offered to us. "God's love was revealed among us in this way: God sent his only Son into the world so that we might live through him. In this is love, not that we loved God but that he loved us and sent his Son to be the atoning sacrifice for our sins."[33]

Scottish broadcaster and writer Alastair Moffat described the difference between his mother and his father in this way: She loved first and asked questions later. He asked questions and then, if the right answers were given, might love his kids. Or as a Hasidic master once described the difference between a God of Love and a god who loves: "Would that I loved the greatest saint as much as God loves the greatest sinner."[34]

We can't "reciprocate" God-love; we can only respond to God-love. To love as God loves—the God-love of forgiveness, grace, hope, sacrificial giving—is not possible without God's power.

Writer Maya Angelou tells the impact of this God-love relationship in her own life:

> One day the teacher, Frederick Wilkerson, asked me to
> read to him. I was twenty-four, very erudite, very worldly.
> He asked that I read from *Lessons in Truth,* a section
> which ended with these words: "God loves me." I read
> the piece and closed the book, and the teacher said,
> "Read it again." I pointedly opened the book, and I sar-
> castically read, "God loves me." He said, "Again." After
> about the seventh repetition I began to sense that there

might be truth in the statement, that there was a possibility that God really did love me. Me, Maya Angelou. I
suddenly began to cry at the grandness of it all. I knew
that if God loved me, then I could do wonderful things,
I could try great things, learn anything, achieve anything.
For what could stand against me with God, since one
person, any person with God, constitutes the majority?[35]

Until it becomes personal, love is no more tangible than a nice
idea, no more powerful than an intriguing theory. Just as God is not
"a Being" but "Being itself," so God is not "a Being that loves" but
"Being Love." God as the Supreme Source of "Being Love" is a pleas-
ant thought, but it is nothing more than that until belief changes to
faith through direct experience.

Belief is saying "I believe in a loving God." Faith is saying "Jesus
loves me this I know."

Belief says, "God is Love." Faith says, "God loves me."

Faith sings, "I am so glad that Jesus loves me, Jesus loves me, Jesus
loves me. I am so glad that Jesus loves me, Jesus loves even me."[36]

Whenever I see a list that includes love as one virtue among
many, I freak out. There is no justifiable list that lumps together wisdom, beauty, duty, and love. There is really *only love,* which Paul
makes clear in some of the most famous words ever written: "and the
greatest of these is *love.*"[37] Love is an ontological reality: God's love is
what makes things real and alive. When the Bible says, "God is love,"
it means that where Love is, there is God. It doesn't say, "God is loving," that the chief characteristic of a "Being" is love, but that Being

> It is not, then, that the Eternal Father has fixed an artificial worth upon us, to value us for what we are not.... There are no fictions with God, not even in his generosity. He does not turn a blind eye to our shallowness; he turns a seeing eye on the infinite depth with which he has underlaid it, the love of Jesus Christ his only Son.
>
> —AUSTIN FARRER[38]

itself is Love. And in living a life of love, we also are living a life of truth, because the One who is Love is also Truth.

God's love goes to the greatest lengths, far exceeding the limitations we take for granted. Some have called Michael Jordan the greatest basketball player who ever lived. He scored more than twenty-nine thousand points and won five MVP awards and six NBA championships. But he also set a higher standard for love, at least as it applies to basketball. Until Jordan arrived on the scene, the standard contract for an NBA player included a clause that prevented any off-season basketball participation without approval from team management. Jordan refused to sign any contract that prevented him from playing the game he loved. So Jordan's contract was written differently. His was the first to include what is called the "love of the game" clause. It gave him the freedom to play basketball whenever he wanted, even during the off-season. In the same way God cedes no part of life to an "off-season for love," since the length of God's love has no limit. Why are we so afraid to claim God's limitless love for the world?

> Go after a life of love as if your life
> depended on it—because it does.
>
> —APOSTLE PAUL[39]

Love Cubed by Breadth

Love is all-encompassing. Nothing is left out of the equation. Nothing and no one is out of bounds for love. The whole world is God's "love place."[40] So it's not hard to figure out whom to love. Everyone.

The Temple was God's dwelling place, the habitation of The Presence. But it was a limited and misleading metaphor, for the prophets were constantly reminding Israel that God is not confined to the Temple box: "Thus says the Lord: Heaven is my throne and the earth is my footstool; what is the house that you would build for me, and what is my resting place?"[41] Both sides of the paradox of a God who was both here and everywhere were pulled together by the psalmist: "The Lord is in his holy temple; the Lord's throne is in heaven."[42]

When you are in relationship with someone, little things mean a lot. Like that watch fob of your great-grandfather's; or that sweater of your mother's that she was always trying to put on you when she got cold. These "worthless" things become your life's greatest treasures, your love icons.

When you are in relationship with the Creator of the universe, little things mean a lot. Like that sparrow that falls from the sky. Or that lily in the field. Or that "little one" whom no one else will talk to.

What are your love icons? Do they represent the helpless, the weak, and those who are "worthless" in the eyes of the world? Or are they people and things that have the power to position you to gain a personal advantage?

> Let heart
> be a hut
> thatched with love.
>
> —GUYANESE POET JOHN AGARD[43]

And when it comes to icons, are you ever tempted to collect lack-of-love icons? Do you spend more of your time judging people or loving people? Does your voice put on love gloves when you reach out to those whose lives and words and actions don't reside within the "acceptable" boundaries?

In September 1975, Lynette "Squeaky" Fromme tried to kill the president of the US. She was a misfit. Both her parents rejected her, and she found the father figure she longed for in Charles Manson. When asked why she would take up with someone like him, a crazed murderer, she said: "Whoever loves me first can have my life."[44]

"My beloved friends, let us continue to love each other since love comes from God."[45] Or as Jesus put it, if you only love those who love you, what's the big deal?[46] And if, through the power of the Spirit, you can find it in your heart to love those who reject you and revile you, how much more so God? You can't outlove the Lord.

The needle of our inner compass needs to point in the direction of true north: Jesus the Christ. But if you look closely at any needle that's pointing true north, it trembles. Love trembles because intimacy hurts. Love is painful. The preciousness of love is matched by the precariousness of love. Love can't be controlled, only cultivated.

There is no love without loss of self and loss of control. Love is the hardest thing in the world to get right, because when you give up control you consent to uncertainty and unpredictable outcomes. Yet losing yourself to find yourself is the way of love.

It's also the way of life. Google's success is based on sending people away from its Web site, not toward it. By relinquishing control and empowering others, by letting go and letting users control their own experiences, Google has become one of the greatest success stories in the history of business.

Likewise, love lets its lover hold the reins. As any farmer can tell you, fence in farm animals in tight enclosures and they become nervous. Give them a wide range, though, and they relax and settle down. People are the same way. We need the fresh air and exercise of free will. Think about the best adventures of your life, the great-

> I will give you a new heart and put
> a new spirit in you.
>
> —THE LORD GOD TO THE PROPHET EZEKIEL[47]

est excitement you have experienced. Do these things come about as a result of your insistence on tight control? The phrase *Mission Control* is an oxymoron. To be "in mission" is to be "out of control."

There is another reason love hurts: the strongest heartbeat in The Presence is a sensitivity to suffering. Intimacy hurts, and love demands that we lose ourselves before we can find ourselves. The metanarrative of suffering love is one of the strongest in the Scriptures. Suffering is not to be avoided or even endured, but appropriated as a means of bringing us closer to God, to ourselves, and to one another. By embracing our suffering, the I embraces dignity and grace and enhances human integrity. And when it comes to love, this is the hardest thing to get right.

In an attempt to shield ourselves against uncertainty and pain, we try to riskproof our relationships to make love less trembly. For fifty dollars you can purchase "Love Detector" software (the Windows version) that promises to take the guesswork out of relationships. It uses the same voice-analysis technology used in devices designed to identify potential terrorists. When used on your cell phone it can help you detect whether the person on the other end has a "love voice" or not.

This is not just a gimmick to sell software to timid or paranoid people, and it's much more than simply a metaphor. We know from Scripture that our hearts actually speak. Jesus tells us that our mouth parrots what's in our heart of hearts. Martin Luther called faith "the 'yes' of the heart."[48] The life integrity that love delivers is not only about what happens on the outside; it's a thoroughgoing life—a new, transformed life—that is integral from the inside out. Love is the wound that breaks open the heart, so that a new heart can be born and a whole soul can be awakened. In the Christian metanarrative, everyone with a new identity, integrity, and intimacy functions from a broken heart.

> God gives us the heart to think with, and the light in our heart is a spark of the divine heart.
>
> —PARAPHRASE OF SIRACH 17[49]

The testimony of the Scriptures is this: if you love, your heart will break. The only question is what kind of love will break your heart. Bob Pierce, founder of World Vision, wrote these words on the flyleaf of his Bible: "Let my heart be broken with the things that break the heart of God."[50]

The cross is the ultimate symbol of a broken heart. For on the cross, God's heart broke. The mixture of blood and water that flowed from Jesus' side reveals what really killed Jesus—a broken heart. Today there is a medical event called "broken heart syndrome." A broken heart can kill you, or it can birth in you a new heart. Jesus' broken heart birthed a new humanity. The promise of The Presence is that it takes a heart broken by love to birth God's love and make the heart beat in sync with God's heart.[51]

> To love at all is to be vulnerable. Love anything and your heart will certainly be wrung and possibly be broken. If you want to make sure of keeping it intact, you must give your heart to no one, not even to an animal.
>
> —C. S. Lewis[52]

The way of the Cross is another way of talking about love's encounter with entrenchments of power and injustice. Jesus defeated principalities and the prince of the power of the air through weakness. He gave up control, giving himself over to death, and in this supreme act of weakness—which also is the supreme act of love—sacrificed himself to overcome the forces of darkness. That's the breadth of love—love without measure.[53]

Love Cubed by Depth

The deeper you go, the holier love gets. The Temple was a place of holiness. The deeper one got into it, the more it became a place of communication, a place where God speaks. The deeper a person went into the Temple, the more holy it got.[54] The problem with the church today is less that it is out of date than it is out of depth.[55]

Part of the integrity of the life of love is that love itself is integral to all of life. Love coheres our existence; it integrates our life. Without the verb of love, life loses cohesion, falls apart.

When you're "in love," everything in the world looks different. Exactly. Love exceeds and reverses the tried and true. Love is a high-standard, depth-sounding word. To believe what is unbelievable, to live what is unlivable, to see what is unseeable, to do what is undoable—these are the deep ways of love. It's time we rise to the occasion and explore love's depths. Only through love do we become more like God.

> What wondrous love is this,
> Oh! my soul! Oh! my soul!...
> What wondrous love is this!
> That caused the Lord of bliss,
> To bear the dreadful curse
> For my soul, for my soul![56]

We've made love into a low-standard word. "Making love" means one-night stands and sex-to-excess. We now fall in and out of love like one falls in and out of bed. We ask, "What's your love interest?" as if love is not a commitment or a passion but merely a passing interest. Our problem is not that people aren't using condoms; our problem is that we treat people like condoms: we use them once and then throw them away. One author has suggested that the patron saint of modern love is not Cupid but Sun-tzu (author of *The Art of War*).[57] Another psychologist argues that love is "a necessary madness,"[58] even "a kind of mental illness" in which we are "afflicted rather than affected by love."[59]

Our current notion of love—an "emotional" state that seizes one's being—is a consequence of modernity.[60] "Love" in Greek *(agape)* is a volitional love, not a feeling love or an emotional love. It is love embodied and enacted that is unconditional, unrestricted, untamed.

The old-fashioned way of love was to choose your love, then love your choice. Or in non-Western cultures, where arranged marriages are still widespread, "have your love chosen for you, then choose to love the one who has been chosen." Likewise, God chooses whom we are to love; then it is up to us to choose to love God's choice for us. And the choice is unlimited—it includes *everyone*. Remember, the dimensions of love are immeasurable.

One of the most incredible verses in the Bible slides right by us: "Jacob served seven years to get Rachel, but they seemed like only a few days to him because of his love for her."[61] Read that again. It doesn't say, "And those seven years were as seven lifetimes." It says those seven years of unrequited love were as seven days. For Jacob, the love itself—not the conquest of the object of his love—was the satisfaction.

British playwright John Mortimer (b. 1923) is confined to a wheelchair due to a series of accidents largely caused by his risk-taking ways. An interviewer playfully asked his wife, Penny, "He really is getting old, isn't he; why do you stay with John? Is it love or duty?" She replied, "Probably both."[62]

> A joyful heart is the normal result
> of a heart burning with love.
>
> —MOTHER TERESA[63]

Postmodern culture can make it harder to love than ever before. In fact, love is made more difficult as the world brings the "yous" closer and closer together. Social psychologist Serge Moscovici calls our society "an institution which inhibits what it stimulates."[64] There is far greater and wider proximity of "others" to love, but much less of what it takes to enable us to love those in close proximity.

Ironically, as we have access to greater material wealth, which enables us to help others, our commitments to one another diminish. The greater our mediated exposure to distant pain and suffering in the world, the smaller our personal investments in ameliorating pain and suffering. The more we see pictures of distant misery and anguish, the more we distance ourselves from misery and anguish. We've never cared so much. We've never done so little.[65]

The lifelong research of physician William Harvey into "The Motion of the Heart and Blood in Animals" inspired Renaissance geologists to posit at the earth's core a central fire that functioned like a heart.[66] In the Jewish tradition, the heart had two chambers, "love like water" and "love like fire." We are "saved" by both water and fire, but prefer the water. With "love like water," love soothes and satisfies. It makes everything grow. But with "love like fire," love burns and sears. Or in the words of the Scriptures, "Love is a flame of the Lord."[67] God's love is white-hot love…not lukewarm love, not ice-cold love, not even "cool" love or "candle" love. Shane Claiborne of The Simple Way likes to say that we are not called to be candles, which can easily be snuffed out, but that we are called to be fire, to be part of what he calls the "Spirit's inferno of love." The fire of love is the fire of God, and to fire up love is to be fired up and to participate in the beating heart that is at the center of the universe.

One of the fire festivals in the Northern European calendar shaped our celebration of Christmas. It was the Norse fire festival of the Yule log, which can also be interpreted as an integrity festival. When the winter solstice became too cold for the great communal gatherings around the large outdoor bonfires that characterized Nordic festivals, families took those communal bonfires into their homes through the Yule log. When the winter was at its worst and the community could not gather together, in the hearth of every home was a symbol of the community, and with the warmth from the giant Yule log, the family felt the midwinter's hope. The tradition was to never let the Yule log be burned completely but to keep it near the hearth so that in a thunderstorm or on the longest night in December, which marked the end of the journey into darkness, it could be lit.[68]

This practice of sharing the warmth of community gets at the real meaning of "eros." When we restrict our understanding of "erotic love" to genital activity, we do a disservice to the Christian tradition. The first Christian commentary on the Song of Songs was written at the beginning of the third century by Hippolytus of Rome. But the most influential treatment of the "Song" was written by Hippolytus's younger contemporary, Origen. In ten books (only three of which survive), Origen portrayed "eros" love as a form of divine hot-flashing of the human species. Eros is the energy of creation, a passion for life that is "life-giving" in all human relationships, whether it be parent/child, friend/friend, lover/lover, person/creation. Eros is an understanding of the divine image in every soul that makes us all conceivers (not consumers). In all our relationships we are designed by God for the conception (not consumption) of life, to conceive in every relationship beauty, truth, and goodness as a reflection of the divine imprint.[69]

To live in The Presence is to conceive new life. Is new life being conceived in each one of your relationships? Only by eros is the soul's union with God enkindled. Eros is the force that draws all things unto God.

"Our God is a consuming fire," the writer of Hebrews declared.[70] Does that "consuming fire" dwell in you—the fire that burned on Mount Sinai, the fire that burned the bush but did not consume it? We are saved by the fire, saved "so as by fire."[71] Fire burns away that which is not pure. The fire is not to be feared; the evil is to be feared. God will not burn us more than we can bear. But we will be burned.

Are you inviting the burning of God? Has the fire invaded your darkness and possessed your soul? Do you keep the sacred fires burning? Fire shows itself as light, the creative energy of God we know as love. Are you on fire with that consuming fire of love? Do lightning strikes of The Presence thunder from your presence?

> Joy is a net of love by which you can catch souls.
>
> —MOTHER TERESA[72]

THE DRAMA OF THE PRESENCE

If someone asks, "What are you going to do today?" how do you respond? Or if someone asks, "How do you wish to treat others?" what do you say? Do you answer, "God"? Has God, love as a verb with a capital L, become the driving *activity* in your life? Not just a principle or a concept, but an active force? Is "God" what you do every day?

The word *drama* comes from a Greek word that means "to do." The Presence is all about God's drama. God didn't just say, "I love you"; God loved. God lived in our midst and loved us. Thomas Aquinas, whom some argue stands as the greatest theologian in

Christian history, proposed that it might be more theologically correct to render the word *God* grammatically as a verb than a noun.[73]

In the language of faith, it takes more than three words to say, "I love you." It takes *all* the words in our life's vocabulary, since love is command central for all of life. Or said another way, love doesn't take words at all, it takes actions and faith. The world needs more wordless love, more true drama.

The Golden Rule is said to be a command: love your neighbor. Jesus' New Commandment—that we are to love others as Christ has loved us—is also a command.[74] But how can you command love?[75] You cannot command an attitude or an emotion, but you can command an action. You can direct a drama. God doesn't command us to be loving or to feel loving, but to love. Period. There is no law on the books of civil society that commands love. There is no principle of philosophy that makes love a command. Only God does.

The world doesn't need more prima donnas, but it does need more drama queens. The God who is a verb issues the command to love. The drama of The Presence turns all of us into love's "drama queens."

6

"YOU"

Receiving a New Intimacy

He who says, "What is thine is thine and
what is mine is thine," is a saint.
—SAYINGS OF THE FATHERS

W hen love moves from I to you, you get soul. Or put
another way, there is no identity with integrity without
intimacy.

Christianity is the religion of the I, but it quickly becomes the
religion of the you. In fact, Christianity is best described as a first-
person faith that puts the second person first. Especially the last
person.

Christianity learned this from its parent. The first paragraph of
the Shema[1] is in the singular and is addressed to the individual: "with

all *your* heart." The second paragraph[2] is in the plural and is addressed to the Hebrew people as a whole.[3] Scripture tells us the I is not good by itself. "It is not good for the man to be alone,"[4] God said in Genesis. "It is not good for Adam to be alone."

> You can have everything under the tree that you ever wanted. And if you're sitting there alone, you are the saddest, loneliest human being on the planet, and there is absolutely nothing that money can buy that will fill your soul.
>
> —ACTRESS JAMIE LEE CURTIS[5]

None of us is capable of going it alone. Not even the US can go it alone in today's world. The price for going it alone is to be left alone. William Maxwell's award-winning novel *So Long, See You Tomorrow* describes urban centers such as New York City as "a place where one can weep on the sidewalk in perfect privacy."[6]

THE SINGLETON SOCIETY

When I was on a preaching mission in South Korea, I thought I might tell a humorous story highlighting the church's loss of its reason for being. But first I tried it out on my translator. The story goes like this:

> A little girl was given her birth certificate to take to her new school. "Be sure not to lose it," her mother said. "Your teacher needs to see it so you can join the class. But you must bring it home."
>
> Of course, the inevitable happened. The little girl lost her birth certificate, and on her way home she sat down and cried, afraid to tell her mother what happened. When someone saw her crying and asked what was wrong, she answered: "I just lost my excuse for being born."

When I asked my translator what he thought, he said, "I don't get it."

"What do you mean you don't get it?" I replied. "That's what has happened to many of our churches: we've lost our 'excuse' for being born."

"I still don't get it," he persisted.

It dawned on me that "getting" the story pivoted on the concept of a birth certificate. "You do have birth certificates in Korea, right?"

"No, I don't really know what you are talking about. What's a birth certificate?"

"When every individual is born, you get some kind of document, right, some paper that proves you were born on such-and-such a date in such-and-such a place, and you keep that paper and use it to get such things as passports?"

"No, we don't have any such thing in Korea."

I decided to start over: "Okay, when a baby is born, what happens?"

"When parents give birth to a child, that child's name is added onto the family of record."

In the West, every child enters life legally defined as a separate entity. In the East, every child enters life legally defined by the network of relationships into which one is born. In some African cultures (for example, speakers of Chichewa, a Bantu language), a child does not achieve "moral" standing until he is "presented" to the community. Until an infant is introduced into relations with others, he has no "moral arrival," only a biological arrival. If an infant dies before being "shown," he is buried without mourning or ceremony. But if an infant emerges from privacy with his mother and is presented to the community, he receives all the privileges of any other person in that community. Long ago, African theologian John Mbiti introduced the West to what he believes is the greatest contribution of Africa to global spirituality, the Ubuntu principle of "I am because we are."[7]

The greatest spiritual heresy of our day is the notion that we are separate from one another, that I can function in this world without you, that I can cry "in perfect privacy." Even Jesus said, "I and my Father are one."[8] Jesus never acted or spoke alone. The creeds begin with "I believe." But Jesus begins, "Our Father..."

Not one of the disciples took Jesus aside and asked, "Teach *me* to pray." Rather than solicit a unique, "I'm-special" personalized prayer, the disciples asked Jesus to teach *us* to pray.[9] They asked for a prayer in common. They asked for the good of their brothers and sisters. It has often been said that in the Lord's Prayer, I is silent. We don't pray alone.[10]

The apostle Paul put it as bluntly as he could: no one can say to anyone else, "I have no need of you."[11] In the you—the other—is the realm of the soul. Loss of connection with the you is another name for loss of soul. People, congregations, and nations can lose their soul. Nothing sucks out the soul faster than when the mouth opens to say, "Leave me alone."

In one episode of *Sex and the City,* Carrie Bradshaw buys a pair of five-hundred-dollar shoes. She tells an amazed friend who has two kids, "I can spend this kind of money on my shoes because that's the choice I've made: to be single." She's sadly mistaken. No one is "made" to be single. We were all "made" for each other—for love relationships with God, with creation, and with others.[12]

One Talmudic reading of the "rib" from which Eve was made is *face.* "The first Adam had two faces. The second Adam encounters his friend, made from his face, face to face."[13] The I becomes truly itself only in communion, only in you. In the other, we see something that reminds us of intimacy, of connection.

One of the greatest things ever written on the Trinity was penned by Gregory of Nazianzen: "I cannot think of the One without immediately being surrounded by the radiance of the Three; nor can I discern the Three without at once being carried back to the

One."[14] In human life as well as divine life, two is really one, and one is really two. Love needs two. When love is only one, there is sickness, a homesickness, even a sickness unto death.

> There are not five or six wonders
> of the world but only one alone: love.
>
> —JACQUES PREVERT[15]

"IF I WERE YOU..."

In philosophy and history there is something called "counterfactual reasoning."[16] It posits alternative scenarios, sudden contingencies, "what if" stories, either for the past or for the future. A textbook example of counterfactual reasoning is the hypothesis "If I were you..."

How good are you at counterfactuals? Can your church do "If I were you" reasoning? In The Presence, where identity has integrity, the I becomes you.

Nothing blocks creativity and conversion more than the failure to do counterfactuals. Psychologist Howard Gardner has discovered there is an inverse relationship between being blind to others while seeing only your own point of view and the ability to change your mind and be creative.[17] Putting yourself in the place of the other, being able to engage in "If I were you…" thinking, opens your life to change and creativity.

Some of the most famous words of the Torah are these: "Now the LORD had said unto Abram, Get thee out of thy country, and from thy kindred, and from thy father's house."[18] We translate the Hebrew *lekh lekha* as "Get thee." But it literally means "Go to thyself." One Hasidic master, Yehudah Laib Alter, the Gerer Rebbe who authored *Sefat Emet*, argued that the phrase *lekh lekha* is best understood to mean "Go out to find yourself."[19]

Unless the I becomes you, the I never truly finds itself and thinks it is dreaming great things when it is really only dozing and daydreaming. When "what's in it for me?" becomes the primary question of life, when feathering your own nest is the ultimate feather in your cap, your whole life comes into question. Without interconnection, life ends with no integrity of identity.

Every day I try to ask my kids a question (especially when they're watching television or playing video games): "What have you done today to bring peace and goodwill into the world?" There can't be peace and joy in the world for me unless there is peace and joy in the world for you. All wars are civil wars. All immorality began with Cain's question, "Am I my brother's keeper?"[20]

Jesus taught counterfactuals through his storytelling. Take the parable of the good Samaritan. When we read that story, we like to see ourselves as the good Samaritan. But the one who stops and stoops to help, the one who bears the full cost of recovery, is not us. The good Samaritan is Jesus.

We are the needy, wounded ones stranded on the highway. And

when we do offer help to those in need, we do so out of an I that has become a you. Or in the powerful words of Hebrews: "Visit those in prison as if in prison with them. Care for the sick because you are still in the body."[21]

Here is the statement that cannot be made in truth: "I have no need of you."[22]

The rich can't say that to the poor.

The learned can't say that to the simple.

The healthy can't say that to the sick.

The strongest nation in the world can't say that to the rest of the world.

I can't say that to you, and you can't say that to me.

In the arena of The Presence, "If one member suffers, all suffer together with it; if one member is honored, all rejoice together with it."[23] Or in words with less authority but more acquaintance, John Donne's words have been widely quoted, but only the last portion. This seventeenth-century poet, who might have been the first Christian writer to show how spiritual love ennobles and elevates sexual love,[24] portrayed the web of connectedness in this way: "Any man's death diminishes me, because I am involved in Mankind, and therefore never send to know for whom the bell tolls: it tolls for thee."[25]

THE SYNERGY OF TWO

Where there is two, there is always three. How can this be?

First, one is really two when the "one" is in relationship with itself, conscious of itself and realizing its self. Second, there is the synergy of two, the mystery of multiples (I and you), a mystery that Jesus conveyed in his fuzzy logic of "two-or-three." Jesus took a tradition from Ecclesiastes—"Two are better than one.... Woe to one who is alone and falls and does not have another to help."[26] He transformed that tradition into a spiritual maxim: "Where two or three are gathered in my name, I am there among them."[27] Synergy means one plus one equals more than two. That's why Jesus' "two or three" phrase nicely conveys life's relationship rule.[28] G. K. Chesterton once said there was more difference between two and three than between three and three million.[29]

The mystery of two is best conveyed in German, where *Zwei* means two and *Zweifel* means doubt. Whenever one becomes two-plus, there's uncertainty and doubt. Relationships are difficult. Asked if he was married, Kazantzakis's (à la Cacoyannis) Zorba the Greek replied, "Wife, children, house—the full catastrophe."[30] Relationships are full of missed connections, mistimed cues, misinterpreted signs, "full catastrophes." Relationships generate uncertainty and unpredictability and vulnerability.[31]

I question people who say, "I just love to write." I want to say, "Are you crazy? Do you ever write?" No one I know who writes "loves to write." Toward the end of his life, historian Charles Beard is supposed to have said that writing is like dragging a cat backward by the tail across the rug: it has never been easy. Writing is hours spent chained to a chair in tedious, hair-pulling, hair-splitting, key-banging labor. Writers don't enjoy writing. Writers enjoy having written.

It is the same with people who say, "I just love to love." Really? Love is hard. Love is tiresome. Lovers don't enjoy loving. Lovers enjoy having loved and being loved. "Only connect!' is E. M. Forster's prescribed solution.[32] But "Only connect!" may be the hardest commandment of all to keep.

Lovers will cry (Jesus did over his best friend, Lazarus).[33] Lovers will be lonely and afraid (Jesus was in the Garden of Gethsemane).[34] Lovers will get furiously angry (Jesus did in the Temple).[35] Lovers will be rejected and betrayed (Jesus was by Judas, Peter, and if truth be told, all the disciples). Lovers will be misunderstood (Jesus was almost constantly). Love and loss go together like sauce and stain. Intimacy means that we love others amid loss, and our losses are huge: abandonment, betrayal, death, failure, guilt, heartache, jealousy, poverty, rage, sorrow. The list goes on and on.

Today, intimacy is not about sharing space and sharing desires and sharing missions. It is about sharing of self, talking about yourself, and baring of bodies.[36] As late as the 1950s, it was considered bad form (in the "advice literature") to talk about yourself or to reveal too much about yourself. Now it's a positive virtue to reveal your deepest self. Even tough guys like Tony Soprano do it. What was said of the marriage of two of the twentieth century's greatest poets, Sylvia Plath and Ted Hughes—"drowning in intimacy, they couldn't rediscover separateness without separating"[37]—could be said of our autistic culture, which is totally absorbed in the self. The Catholic Church calls it "The American Impediment." One of the most common "grounds" for granting annulments in the US is what the church calls male "psychological impotence," an inability to form intimate relational bonds.[38]

We want the intimacy that a child has with her parents, yet we want the freedom and autonomy that an adult has. We don't want to be twisted and tied and caged in covenantal entanglements, yet we are desperately hunting for relationships that are fulfilling and lasting. And guess what that involves? A foundational metanarrative of mutual and covenantal "I love you" entanglements.

Christian publishing houses are flooding the market with books about the need to restructure the church and make it more relevant. The only restructuring we need is not of more relevant organizations but of more just relationships. There is a lot of confusion surrounding the words *just* and *justice*. "They deserve justice" has come to mean "give them what they deserve," a punishment that meets the crime. This is not what the Bible means by justice. In the metanarrative of The Presence, justice is summed up in one word: *intimacy*. And, specifically, intimacy as it relates to three relationships. Biblical justice is a relationship of intimacy with creation, a relationship of intimacy with one another, and a relationship of intimacy with God. For some, Jesus comes to show the way to heaven from earth. For others, he comes to show the way to heaven on earth. For those in The Presence, Jesus comes to show both.

In our restructured relationships, we need the just intimacy of the three essential yous:

1. You of God Intimacy. Can we love God with the whole heart?
2. You of Others Intimacy. Can we cherish one another as an I—as another self? Can we love a neighbor as much as we love ourselves?

3. You of Creation Intimacy. Can we live the reality that "the earth is the LORD's" and not ours—and that we have been commissioned to care for God's earth?

As far as in us lies, in our acre of earth, can the kingdom come? Can The Presence be known and made manifest on Earth? Can we love God above all else, love others like they are another I, and love the earth and all things in it?

> Divine justice demands that I love.
>
> —FATHER WALTER J. BURGHARDT[39]

1) Intimacy with the You of God

In terms of his ability to discover and dream, Isaac Newton has only two peers in history: Leonardo da Vinci and Albert Einstein. By the time he was twenty-three, Newton had turned the scientific world of his day on its head. In the course of his life the brilliance of his mind led to amazing discoveries in the worlds of science and math[40] and also (and this is less known) in the world of theology.[41] Toward the end of Newton's life, an admirer asked how he was able to discover and do so many incredible things. Newton's answer: "By always thinking upon them."[42]

When I read that, it reminded me of something Mabel Boggs Sweet used to do. An ordained minister in the Pilgrim Holiness Church, my mother had the annoying habit of humming when she was doing housework or running errands. One day I asked her, "Mom, why are you humming?" She replied, "I'm thinking about Jesus." I said, "It sounds to me like you're humming, not thinking." She smiled and said, "I'm thinking by humming. Can't you hear what I'm humming?"

She then began to sing what I recognized as one of her favorite songs:

> Jesus is all the world to me,
> My life, my joy, my all;
> He is my strength from day to day,
> Without Him I would fall.
> When I am sad, to Him I go,
> No other one can cheer me so;
> When I am sad, He makes me glad,
> He's my friend.[43]

On what am I always thinking? Each one of us daydreams, and these dreams shape the metanarratives of our daily lives. One of the recurrent entries in the diary of the second president of the United States, John Adams, went something like this: "At home with my family. Thinking." or "At home. Thinking."[44]

What are we thinking?

In Ephesians, Paul defines the ultimate spiritual practice using just three words: "Walk in love."[45] To walk with Jesus is to walk in love. And that "daily walk" is shaped by our daydreams, which tell us of the "desires of the heart." These desires shape our destiny.[46] Are we daydreaming of hitting it big in the lottery, hitting a home run at work, at school, at church, or hitting the bulls-eye of the USAmerican Dream? Or do our daydreams walk in love? Are my daydreams like Mabel's? "Jesus is all the world to me, my life, my joy, my all"?[47]

When someone asks, "What are you thinking about?" or "What do you think about?" can you say, "I'm thinking about Jesus"?

When we walk with Jesus, we find that the walk has different gaits: sometimes a run, sometimes a dance, sometimes a saunter, sometimes a limp, sometimes a rest. But is that "daily walk" one of intimacy with God? The study of the Scriptures is the highest form of "you of God" intimacy. To be in relationship with the Scriptures is not obedience to a commandment (a mitzvah); rather it is to be ushered into the presence of God, as close to God as we shall ever get outside of being in God's direct presence in heaven.

Trahit sua quemque voluptas.
"We all do what we want."

—VIRGIL, *ECLOGUES*[48]

2) Intimacy with the You of Others

One of the ministers of a local church was delivering meals as part of his volunteer work with a Meals On Wheels mission. He took a meal to the home of a woman whose only child was visiting that day. The man congratulated the woman for having such a nice son and added, "I have eight children of my own."

"Eight kids!" exclaimed the woman. "I love my son so much that I can't imagine dividing love by eight."

"Ma'am," the man said gently, "you don't divide love—you multiply it."

Jesus love is not zero-based, in which the more you give the less you have left. Jesus love is eternity-based: the more you give, the more there is to go around. Jesus love is infinity-based: true love defies gravity.[49] You get more the more you give away. In the calculus of love, you can't possess what you don't give away.

Jesus love is other-based: we are to reach out in love to "all" people and "especially [to] those of the family of faith."[50] In the words of one biblical scholar, "The Christian community...defines only the minimum of love's responsibility, not its farthest extent."[51] The Jesus who is of one substance with the Father wants to be of one substance with every human being, and he wants *us* to be of one substance with every human being. Only in relationship with the "you" of others can we experience ourselves moving from quasi selves to quality selves and true selves.

In her wonderful book on the Lord's Prayer, Lorraine Kisly says that while we might pray the "Our Father" in church on Sunday, we

actually are living a prayer that "turns the Lord's Prayer on its head."
She suggests that this is the actual prayer of our hearts when we recite
the "Our Father":

> Master of Earth,
> Exalt my name over all others.
> Give me a kingdom where my will is never
> thwarted.
> Let me take whatever I wish, and grant me
> vengeance over all who oppose me.
> Let me satisfy my every desire,
> And give me the power to crush anyone
> who stands in my way.[52]

The praying of an external "Our Father," Kisly writes, is our protection "from the infernal prayer that tempts all of us, always, at
every moment."[53]

*Dans l'adversité de nos meilleurs amis, nous
trouvons quelque chose qui ne nous déplaît pas.*
"In the adversity of our best friends, we always find
something which is not wholly displeasing to us."

—FRANÇOIS, DUC DE LA ROCHEFOUCAULD[54]

The poet James Fenton was tired of writing about being "in love." So he let the phrase "in Paris" stand in and do work for the phrase "in love."

> Don't talk to me of love. Let's talk of Paris.
> I'm in Paris with the slightest thing you do.[55]

What if we exchanged the phrase "in love" not with "in Paris" but with "in Christ." After all, for a Christian, intimacy is being "in Christ" with the other. It's not two people gazing at each other, but both gazing in the same direction "in Christ," both working to turn daydreams into God dreams for the church and the world.

Conviviality is not a word one hears much anymore, but it's a word worth reclaiming. The first syllable in *convivial* means "together"; the *vivial* comes from *vivere,* which means "live." *Convivial* means "live together." Christians are by definition convivial. Christians either learn to live convivially or die trying.

In the act of communion, we liturgically express most intimately our conviviality (living together). We come together in thanksgiving both for our life in Christ and our life together. My friend Chuck Conniry, who heads up the doctor of ministry program at George Fox University, tells the story of being in the midst of a communion service where the bread was so stale and the grape juice so flat that his mouth and soul both recoiled in horror at the travesty of our treatment of Jesus' body and blood. But suddenly the Spirit spoke a word of rebuke to him: in the bread of Christ we taste a dry, broken, and betraying body of Christ so that we may know the way God finds us and still loves us—a dry, broken, betraying body of Christ. That's why the church has historically begun the Eucharist with these words of honesty and self-revelation:

> Ye that do truly and earnestly repent of your sins, and
> are in love and charity with your neighbors, and intend
> to lead a new life, following the commandments of God,
> and walking from henceforth in his holy ways; draw
> near with faith, and take this holy sacrament to your
> heart.[56]

Some of the biggest fights in church history have occurred over how Christ is present in the Eucharist. But the real issue is not how Christ is present in the Eucharist, but how Christ is present in us and how we are present to others. How do we become a Eucharistic presence to others? How can we, who are dry, broken, and betraying, become "Eucharists," The Presence for the world.

How do we become "present" for The Presence? An old heresy says we can do this only when we get away from the world and its distractions. Want to meet Jesus? Put some distance between you and the pace and politics of life. Go meditate somewhere. Go contemplate somewhere.

That's not what Jesus taught. He said The Presence is encountered in the yuckiness and muckiness of life.

George Fox, the founder of the Quakers, said there is "that of God" in every person.[57] Whether the person saw it or not, or whether he liked it or not, "that of God" was there. That's why Fox didn't found a new religion, but a Society of Friends.[58]

While The Presence can be found in every you—indeed, every human bears the image of God—The Absence emanates from every you as well. In God's incarnational embrace of humans, Christ frees us to love others. But God's embrace does not remove the splinters from our personalities or erase all enraged, deranged, unbalanced perspectives. Is there anyone who honestly would make a good "character witness" for himself?

Relationships are as much bitterness and dark as sweetness and light. There is a lot of romanticism and idealism in current writing on "community"—especially from the communitarians, who are hankering after the imagined stable communities of the past. But bonding can quickly become bondage. As the nineteenth-century French social observer Alexis de Tocqueville warned, there is no tyranny like the tyranny of the majority. Just challenge the common will of a community and find out the strength of invisible chains.

Some Christians are guilty of a realized eschatology. They expect things to be as perfect in the here-and-now as in the sweet bye-and-bye. Christians don't live "one world at a time." Christians live the world to come in the world that is. But in the world that is, every you goes from feeling like a proper noun (the honored You) to feeling like a petty, piddling adjective (every you has fat-and-ugly attacks). What's more, every you does some "stinkin' thinkin'," as it's called in the black church.

> Those who are in love with community,
> destroy community; those who
> love people, build community.
>
> —Dietrich Bonhoeffer[59]

Every you knows firsthand the truth if not the words of the old hymn:

Two wonders I confess:
The wonders of His glorious love
And my unworthiness.[60]

Every you lives the simultaneous reality of saint and sinner. I am beautiful, and the ugliness is me. Both are true. Every you is beautiful to God, because every you is a divine creation. In the world we now live in, I am not beautiful in and of myself. I am miserable. I malfunction. Jesus is my only Beauty.

Put as much padding as possible between saint and sinner, and you still end up with both bumping into each other. Sin and virtue are natural bedfellows. Hormones push us one way, holiness another. In the world we're in, every you lives out the struggle between the lower and the higher forces. The barbarians may be at the gate, but they're on both sides of it.[61] God made me to do good. But "what I do is not the good I want to do."[62] In the words of the country-and-western song, "Wrong's What I Do Best."[63]

When others do wrong to us, we can do right by imagining two images: a bucket and a spiral staircase. The bucket image comes from Neil Wyrick, who recommends that we imagine we have a bucket of liquid love. When someone does wrong to us, we pour that bucket all over him until "the love lay in puddles at the man's feet."[64]

The second image comes from one of Dutch artist M. C. Escher's lithographs. At best, life is like ascending Escher's unending spiral staircase.[65] We climb round and round, repeating the same mistakes, taking detours on the downward curve before ascending once again. Sometimes we slump up the stairs, sometimes we slide down the stairs, yet we pick up wisdom on the path and gradually ascend from the darkness.

On our oxbow journey, there is no such thing as people "of no importance." In fact, our best steps forward are propelled by contact with other yous who are struggling up the stairs. Everything we do—our learning, our strivings, our dreaming and daydreaming—needs to be shaped by the one in three people who live on less than two dollars per day. We need to be shaped by the ten thousand Africans who die of AIDS, TB, and malaria every day, and the fifty million people who die of hunger every year. That's why the condition of our souls has a direct relation to the condition of our neighborhoods and our nations. Something is wrong when the wealth of some depends on the poverty of others. Something is wrong when the ascent up the ladder for some depends on the descent down the ladder for others.[66]

3) Intimacy with the You of Creation

Have you heard the story of the duck that wanted grapes?[67]

> A duck waddles into a convenience store, hops up onto the counter, and says to the guy working there, "Got any grapes?"
>
> The guy says, "I'm sorry. We don't have grapes."
>
> The duck nods, hops off the counter, and waddles out.
>
> The next day, the duck comes back, hops onto the counter, and asks, "Got any grapes?"
>
> The guy sighs and says, "Let me explain. This is a convenience store. We don't carry produce. So no, I don't have grapes."
>
> Again, the duck nods, hops off the counter, and waddles out.
>
> Back he comes the next day, hops onto the counter, and asks, "Got any grapes?"
>
> Now the convenience store guy is exasperated. "Listen, I explained to you that this store doesn't carry grapes. And if you ask me one more time I'll nail those stupid feet of yours to this counter."
>
> The duck nods, hops down, and waddles out.
>
> The next day, the duck waddles in again, hops onto the counter, and asks, "Got any nails?"
>
> The guy behind the counter takes a deep breath and

says, "You would really need to find a hardware store for that. No, I don't have any nails."

The duck nods and says, "Good. Got any grapes?"

The duck was not going to be educated about convenience stores. And church culture seems dead set against being educated about the environment and what it takes to care for it. It's time to reconsider a strategy that has failed. Why not, instead of trying to convince the church that the care of creation is biblical and essential, simply try to care for creation? Instead of berating the church for not taking a lead in the protection of God's handiwork, it's time to mend the broken connections with one another and with God's garden planet. After all, isn't that what God originally designed us to do: tend and till the garden.[68]

The etymological root of the word *paradise* is "garden." *Paradise* is derived from Old Persian *pairidaeza* (*pairi*, "around"; *daeza*, "wall"), which refers to the sixth-century-BC enclosed park for hunting and tree cultivation.[69] There actually exists a gardener's job description written in ink on a jar from Hellenistic Egypt dated to the late third century AD. The gardener's name is Peftumont, and his daily duties are as follows: first, "water the garden and maintain its irrigation channels"; second, "make four baskets of palm fibre for earth"; third, protect the garden against destructive invasions (for example, sparrows and crows); and fourth, "complete his work at the end of each day." There was one more thing: Peftumont was required to "hand over his own excrement for inspection, so that Talames [his employer] may 'probe it with a stalk' to ensure the gardener had not eaten the produce of the garden." One wonders how often Talames exercised this right of inspection.[70]

Like Talames's claim of ownership to the garden that Peftumont tended, the planet we live on is God's garden: "The earth is the LORD's, and the [fullness] thereof."[71] But unlike Talames, who forbade his gardener from tasting of its fruits, God expects us to enjoy the fullness of the garden, the fullness of air, sea, sky, and soil. In God's garden, we find every good thing[72] to help us overcome obstacles and to inspire us to move forward and upward.

But the rest of the gardener's ancient job description still holds. In a world more familiar with outlets than outdoors, in a world more "logged in" to blogs and vlogs than trees and topiaries, we are to care for the garden's long-term preservation. It takes about one hundred years to produce an inch of topsoil, and you can lose it all in one bad gale or through the neglect of one bad gardener.

An intimate relationship with God's handiwork means that every Christian is a regionalist. To know the part (region) is to know the whole (universe), and vice versa. A responsibility to care for your part of the whole extends to being responsible for the whole. Because you hold your piece of the action, your piece of the whole, you can't hold your peace. You can't stand by and watch as the planet is damaged and scarred and as people are starving and dying. Intimacy with the you of God's handiwork conscripts us all into "farmer-poet Wendell Berry's 'I stand for what I stand on'-ism."[73]

In D. H. Lawrence's *Sons and Lovers* (1913), the central character, Paul, berates his girlfriend, Miriam, for what he sees as her neediness and vulnerability. He gets enraged when "she bent and breathed a flower" because "it was as if she and the flower were loving each other. Paul hated her for it. There seemed a sort of exposure about the action, something too intimate." The world needs more intimacies of bending and breathing a flower.[74]

The yew tree provides one of my favorite metaphors for intimacy with the you of creation. Yew trees grow upward for the first few hundred years. But the older they get, the more time they spend growing outward, creating a green umbrella scattered with red beads. The yew creates a dark canopy under which children love to play and hide. The most aged of yews, hunchbacked and bent to the ground, put down fresh roots from their own dying branches, thereby generating new life out of their own compost.

It is one thing for natural climate changes to turn Egypt from a well-watered environment to a desert. It is another thing for humans to turn the North and South Poles from icecaps to hot tubs. Too often religion has been an environmentally destructive force. Jared Diamond has shown how religious motivation lay behind the deforestation of Easter Island. To transport and erect the giant stone statues that were worshiped there, Easter Islanders cut down their beautiful trees, which led to the environmental and then economic and cultural breakdown of their civilization.[75] Environmental devastation can no more be a good thing than war in the Middle East can be a good thing. We pray for a new heaven and the new earth, but never do we think of destroying heaven to get a "new heaven." Why do we think we have the right to destroy earth to get a "new earth"?

THE WAY OF I-YOU LOVE

Worship is not an annihilation of the I or an absorption of the I into The Presence. Worship is the hyphenating of the three hardest words into the holy mystery of one word: "I-love-you."

The ultimate problem we have in these three words is a problem of grammar. "I" is the subject. "Love" is the verb. "You" is the object. Whenever we treat "you" as objects and not as subjects, we compromise the gospel. Whenever we see things as apart from ourselves and not as parts of ourselves, we compromise a gospel that knows no objects, only subjects. It would be better if we were to live according to I-you love, rather than I-love-you.

With I-you love, we accept the responsibility God has given us by loving us first. Because I am loved by God, and *only* because of God's love, I can love others. I can love the you of God, the you of other people, and the you of God's creation. In the words of Scripture, "We love because he first loved us."[76] We cannot ignore the power of this truth. We have not been left on our own to figure out how to get the three hardest words in the world right. God took the initiative by choosing to love us first, and God is our Mentor and Teacher, helping us with the daunting challenge of practicing the three hardest words.

We'll never say the words perfectly ourselves. But at least we can try. And when we don't get these three words right, we can remember the metanarrative: God so loved the world; Christ so redeemed the world; the Spirit so pervades the world: So *what* are we worried about?

APPENDIX

MANIFOLD WITNESS

To the weak I became weak,
to win the weak.
—APOSTLE PAUL

There is one gospel and one name by which we must be saved.[1] But each culture will incarnate the gospel in its own way. This is not syncretism but the authentic expression of people who come to know God in a way that is true to their world and life experience.

Paul understood this better than anyone. In his mission to take the gospel to the Gentile world, he was a master at finding common ground on which to build a meaningful gospel proclamation—even to the point of quoting pagan poets.[2] And outside the Gentile world, when he was interacting with Jews, he "became like a Jew, to win the Jews."[3] So as we think about an authentic gospel witness in light of the biblical practice of the three hardest words, it is necessary to think about "you" within the context of each person's culture, history, and life experience.

IN MANIFOLD WITNESS

It is perhaps the greatest discovery of the human genome project.[4] The more we look at life on the genetic level, the more similar living things appear. But the more we look at life from ground level, the more diverse living things seem to behave.

Our soulscape reflects our landscape. The more the connective self inhabits The Presence, and the Presence inhabits our midst, the more dissimilar we become from one another. When we wear the face of Christ, our true face emerges and the uniqueness of our I shines.

The mirror of Christ is like a gigantic mirror-ball: shine a light on it from different angles and it will reflect something different back. A very old Jewish regulation requires that every synagogue have twelve windows representing the twelve tribes of Israel. Each tribe has its own window to heaven, and each of the windows has a slightly different vantage point.

We need to resist the pressures that would force us into an identical mold. As the old saying goes, People are equal but not similar. And as the New Testament teaches, God has arranged us with our differences in mind—an eye here, a nose there, a foot or a hand somewhere else.[5] Jesus makes us wholly who we are—each one of us.

There is no greater testimony to the dangers of a false self and a fake I than the creeping sameness in both humans and nature.

Humorist Will Rogers is alleged to have said, "If you and I are exactly alike, then one of us is unnecessary." We are fast moving toward a world filled with unnecessary people in an increasingly homogenous world.

Our culture bombards us into conformity through television, movies, books, magazines, radio, newspapers, and blogs. I've even found myself repeating something I'd heard said on television almost verbatim. I thought I was saying something original but then realized I was parroting something I had heard hours earlier on the news. In the words of the proverbial postmodern mother, "Why can't you be a nonconformist, like everybody else?"

> Join with all nature in manifold witness
> To Thy great faithfulness, mercy and love.
>
> —THOMAS O. CHISHOLM[6]

THE MANIFOLD MANIFESTO

One of the greatest challenges of the twenty-first century is the reclaiming of the world's exoticism, an aesthetics of the different. When the whole body becomes one thing nothing works well. Perhaps the greatest failure of the ecumenical movement of the twentieth century was its failure to develop a "manifold witness" that could translate into an authentic Manifold Manifesto for the twenty-first century.

In your car's engine, the manifold is a one-chamber pipe with multiple apertures for making connections. Likewise, a manifold is the interaction of "manywheres," which are not afraid of elsewhere, and which become a whole somewhere. The first Pentecost was a manifold witness where, as described in Acts, members of the early church came from "every nation under heaven."[7] The ecumenical movement was a singular witness where the language of cultural "diversity" was used to enforce theological uniformity; where "tolerance" was a way of imposing a "right-thinking," left-wing orthodoxy. Multicultural language became a cover for monocultural Christianity.

Multiple and Conflicting Identities

A first plank in any Manifold Manifesto might be the recognition that each I is complex, possessing multiple and even conflicting identities. Teresa of Avila, in her spiritual classic *The Interior Castle,* proposed that human identity be envisioned as "a castle made entirely out of a diamond or of very clear crystal, in which there are many rooms, just as in heaven there are many dwelling places."[8] The J. K. Rowling of his day, Arthur Ransome, wrote a letter to Pamela Whitlock advising her about a book project she was working on with Katharine Hull.[9] Ransome's advice was revealing:

> The ONLY audience you have to think about is Pamela. And Pamelas, of course, are like Chinese boxes, one

inside the other. You have to get at the insidest you can and for ever be suspecting that there is yet another inside that.[10]

Our tiered identity is reflected not only in onionskin souls, but in layered local, regional, national, and global affiliations. In fact, we are living in a world where multiple affiliations and hyphenated names are the norm. There are different strata in the soul, and different strata to each soul.

> Gather us in, thou Love that fillest all,
> Gather our rival faiths within the fold,
> Rend each man's temple veil and bid it fall
>
> . . . .
>
> Gather us in.
>
> —BLIND NINETEENTH-CENTURY HYMN
> WRITER GEORGE MATHESON[11]

In 1963, a southern truck driver named Elvis Presley was at the height of his career. Elvis had a magpie mind: he picked up vibrations everywhere he went. His best biographer calls him a "naturally assimilative" stylist with a "multiplicity of voices."[12] While he emulated others' styles, he didn't ventriloquize voices. Whatever style of music he was singing—country, gospel, pop, rhythm and blues—he funneled it through the grid of his I. He enjoyed many different kinds of music and refused to make distinctions between them.

His ability to create musical experiences (as well as his shaking hips) came from black culture; his rapport with his audience, as well as his deep emotional resonances and nuances, came from a gospel quartet called The Statesmen, where lead tenor Jake Hess's controlled vibrato helped Elvis know when to rein in and lead out. His use of costume reflected his intuitive understanding of the power of image. He was not afraid to connect opposites, and he embodied paradox with a pioneering sense of irony.

In short, Elvis was in many ways the first postmodern performer (or at least the first EPIC musician).[13] Elvis never forgot where he came from, but neither did he let where he came from define the limits of who he was or where he was going.

In his magisterial look at *The Ethics of Identity,* Princeton philosopher Kwame Appiah calls this "rooted cosmopolitanism," whereby a person can be a patriot and at the same time a global citizen upholding universal values.[14] If it were all about roots, and not also about rootlessness and cosmopolitanism, we would have not had novelists such as Conrad and Nabokov or preachers like Jesus. Some people need to spend their lives on the same street, in the same city, in the same house, seeing the same views. Others need a variety of vistas.

But the ideal is to be rooted in soul no matter how uprooted you are in place or how global you are in focus. If the military can recognize the value of both roots and wings, why can't the church?[15]

> What should they know of England
> who only England know?
>
> —RUDYARD KIPLING[16]

The Dignity of Difference

A second plank in the Manifold Manifesto is the dignity of difference. We have two Creation accounts, not one, because our lightweight, two-pound box of brains *needs* more than one account. We have four gospels, not one, because we need four. It takes many accounts to help mortals see the incredibly rich picture of who Jesus is. In Matthew, it is the Sermon on the mountain. In Luke, it is the sermon on the plain. These are not contradictions but reflections of the manifold witness. One person's mountain is another person's plain.[17] Just talk to two people, one from Estes Park, Colorado, the other from Elkins, West Virginia.

Every one of us is different, even when we're doing the same thing. A Debussy pianissimo is very different from a Beethoven pianissimo. Debussy is unearthly; Beethoven is physical. Each culture is different, even when it's doing the same thing. Think of images of poverty in Africa: what comes to mind? Think of images of poverty in North America: what comes to mind? "Living in poverty" means different things to different people in different places. Comedian Chris Rock jokes that USAmerica is the only country in the world where the poor people are fat.

A healthy ecosystem needs diversity, which is what makes cloning so dangerous. Cloning is the abolishment of diversity. And think about organizational cloning and social cloning, as segments of our culture celebrate enforced sameness. There needs to be a new Westminster Dog Show that would reward originality, uniqueness, and the breeding for temperament, spirit, and kindness rather than judging a dog on the basis of meeting some abstract, ideal yardstick of uniformity. When any species is bred to cloned standards, the gene pool is being trashed, and the species becomes vulnerable to all sorts of invasions. Sameness is a one-way ticket to extinction.

And then there is the lack of sameness, which often gets people into trouble. Say what you will about the 2005 Michael Jackson trial, but it was as much about being different as it was about pedophilia. Anybody that weird (in the media, Jackson often is referred to as Wacko Jacko), anybody whose life is that much a "freak show," had to be guilty of something. But is it a crime to look weird (notice how the more Jackson tried to eradicate his facial "flaws" and differences, the weirder he looked)? So what if you want to breed tarantulas or even grow tulips (which I find equally strange)?

Sometimes it's our eccentricities that prod us into our greatest contributions. Walt Disney was mortified of mice, and initially named his famous cartoon character Mortimer Mouse after the mouse that terrorized his studio shack when he started out in Kansas City. Elvis had a .357-caliber magnum handy to shoot his television set when Robert Goulet (the symbol of everything Elvis didn't want to be) was singing.[18]

I can hear passionate objections to what I'm saying. An obvious one is: "But what about the beds they slept in?" In previous eras, the household "bed" had more of a social function than a private one. In the medieval world, when the bedding wasn't spread on a bare floor or on rushes, the primary (and often largest) piece of furniture in a house was the bed. It was where everyone lounged together and where the entire household and their guests slept. Just as *companion* originally meant someone who shared bread (*com* means "with"; *panera* means "bread"), *comrade* originally meant someone who shared your bed or tent. And these beds often were filled with "strange bedfellows." Puritan fathers tucked their daughters into the same bed with a boyfriend—but not without putting a bundling board between them. One of the most wrongly maligned people in history is the Bethlehem innkeeper who wasn't so much slamming the door on Mary and Joseph as offering an any-moment mother the only private space he had at his disposal.[19]

Without arguing for the guilt or innocence of Elvis or Michael

> A citizen of the world can make the world better by making some local place better.
>
> —KWAME APPIAH[20]

Jackson or anyone else, the point is that eccentric behavior is not primarily cause for alarm or a reason to banish people—especially from the gospel.

God's Appearance in Various Cultures

A third plank in any Manifold Manifesto is the indigenization of The Presence in every person, in every level of society, in every culture, in every historical era. The primary mentality of the church has been to export Western Christianity to the rest of the world. But Jesus was no Westerner. He speaks to every culture in its own accent. Jesus speaks differently to us in the twenty-first century than he did in the first. Besides, there is a glittering, new world address for Christianity. The lights are dim in the West and the North. The doorbell now rings in the South and East, and the person who typically answers the door is a woman from a Brazilian *favela* (slum) who greets her visitor in Portuguese and who lives a Christian faith with southern-hemisphere concepts and practices.[21] Without enculturation there can be no coherent metanarrative of The Presence.

The best days of Christianity will be found in the future. In fact, in some ways Christianity is just now getting out of diapers and starting to walk. When it starts to run, hold on for dear life. For the promise of the gospel is that one day, Christianity will do more than walk or run: it will fly. And the rapturous ride of a Christ unleashed in the world will be something to experience.

A living faith is like a living person: It keeps growing. It has a capacity for self-renewal *(semper reformanda)* and changes constantly.

We may sing "Gimme that old-time religion," but we don't sing "Lord, return us to the good ole days." We don't pray like Peter Pan, forbidden from growing up, "Lord, keep us in the good old days." We sing and pray for faith that can help us serve "*this* present hour," trusting that the Bible has reference to and relevance for "the living of these days."[22]

> Contact between cultures is the oxygen of civilization.
>
> —AIMÉ CÉSAIRE[23]

DOUBLE ESCHATOLOGY

The Bible teaches a double eschatology that connects the ends of the earth to the end of time. As a spiritual discipline, I try to make the last words of the Bible ("Maranatha" or "Come, Lord Jesus") my first words of the day and a mantra throughout the day.

But the word *maranatha* has two different meanings, depending on how you parse the word:

- "Mara-natha" means "Come Lord" or "Lord come."
- "Maran-atha" means "Lord is here" or "Lord has come."

To be "Rapture ready," Christians need to live both meanings of Maranatha. First, we are to live expectantly for the *parousia* (called in many evangelical circles "the Rapture"—"For the Lord himself, with a cry of command, with the archangel's call and with the sound of God's trumpet, will descend from heaven, and the dead in Christ will rise first. Then we who are alive, who are left, will be caught up in the clouds together with them to meet the Lord in the air; and so we will be with the Lord forever.")[24] This is the traditional meaning of "Come, Lord Jesus!"[25] and an eschatology that looks upward toward Christ's return and the Rapture.

But the second meaning of Maranatha is one that looks outward as well as upward for the embodiment of Christ. Jesus has come. He is here already, inviting us to get "caught up" or "raptured" in the fulfillment of the Great Commission: "Go into all the world and make disciples of all cultures."[26] Mark's version helps us understand that "all cultures" embraces "all creation": "Go into all the world and preach the gospel to all creation."[27] Disciples of Jesus are incarnants, "caught up" in the incarnation of the gospel in all the world's 16,200 people groups.[28] With 6,200 unreached people groups remaining, there is a lot for us to be caught up in.[29]

There is the rapture from above, but there is also the rapture from below. This is the second form of Christ's eschatological "embodiment." In Ephesians, the church as the body of Christ was instructed to grow up to full "stature," and our true humanity is measured by the "full stature" of Christ. In the Greek, the same word is used in Paul's phrase "full stature of Christ" as in Luke's description of Zaccheus as "small in stature." The church began small in stature, but through our being caught up in God's mission in the world and our participation in The Presence, we can body-build the church into the full stature of Christ.

The truth of Jesus was incapable of reaching full stature in the culture in which Jesus lived. That is one reason I say that we live in the most exciting era ever for the church. With the church growing in stature and now starting to walk, it will in the future break into a run. That's why the church's future has never been so full of promise and expectation.

Jesus' relationships with people and with culture were marked by tenderness, patience, and understanding, even in the face of great wrongs and great failures. Take polygamy and slavery, as just two examples. The world into which Jesus came could not conceive of life without slavery. In fact, the ancient economy was based on slavery. Similarly, the ancient family was most often a quadrangle: a husband, a wife, a concubine, and a courtesan. But Jesus, by regulating the way we treat others and how we think about others, led us inexorably into a place where slavery and polygamy were abolished.[30]

Let's talk about a current scourge: the prevalence of racism. I am part of the last generation (the "boomers") that grew up reading the children's picture book *The Story of Little Black Sambo,* first published in 1899. As horrible as that book's stereotypes appear today, the story ironically was designed to paint a positive picture of a black child at a time when it was hard to find black heroes and positive images in popular literature.

Or take the crusade of Derek Walcott to tell the story of Jesus from a noneurocentric context. This Pulitzer Prize–winning poet was a man of mixed race, referred to then as "mulatto." Walcott grew up as an English-speaking Methodist (his mother, Alix, taught in the English Methodist school) in Castries on the Caribbean (and predominantly Catholic) island of St. Lucia. Walcott's powers as a poet have been described as "the greatest of any poet now alive."[31] Both of his grandfathers were of European descent, but both of his grandmothers were of African descent. In the mid-1970s, Walcott tried to get someone to produce a film about Jesus in which Jesus would be portrayed as other than white. The only person he could interest in making the film was soft-core pornographer Russ Meyer.

Christianity can never be fully understood in just one language or in only one culture. All cultures are hearing impaired; all cultures "see through a glass," but dimly.[32] And each dimness is uniquely its own. For the body to achieve its full stature, every body part needs to be "joined and held together by every supporting ligament...as each part does its work."[33] This is the power of Pope John Paul II's memorable metaphor that the separation of Eastern and Western Christianity has meant that the church has been breathing out of "one lung" for too long. Thomas Merton died in Bangkok trying to breathe out of "both lungs," exploring for himself the East-West connection as he advocated in his writings the loosening of the Western collar around the necks of religious leaders. Without Eastern perspectives, Western notions of nature and normality are seriously flawed and reductive.

There are certain aspects to The Presence I will never experience until the gospel is rendered idiomatic for unreached people groups like Khandeshi, Awadhi (Baiswari, Bagheli), Magadhi Bihari

(Maghori)—all in India. For the full stature of the body of Christ to be reached, the incarnation needs to take place in every culture.[34] This is emphatically not a lazy moral relativism that indiscriminately affirms the truth of all cultures or that celebrates every culture just because it's different. But it *is* an incarnational and missional ecclesiology that is reflected in the New Jerusalem, as it is described in the book of Revelation. It will be "from every nation, from all tribes and peoples and languages, standing before the throne and before the Lamb."[35] And what a human rainbow that will be!

The body of Christ is the right metaphor for cross-cultural incarnation. Bodies stay relatively the same, but they look and eat and talk and worship differently. "Taking God's name in vain" is less about swearing than it is about demeaning and degrading the true nature of God. Christians "take God's name in vain" when they aren't at the front lines for preserving native cultures and languages. The loss of languages (sixty-four languages disappear every year)[36] and the loss of cultures, such as the Beothuks (the now-extinct native tribe of Newfoundland) are more than mission malfunctions. Their loss dwarfs the body of Christ, handicapping it from reaching full stature.

Christians take God's name in vain when they confuse "Christianization" with "Westernization." Alas, when too many people around the world think of Christianized countries, they think first of imperialism, colonialism, materialism, consumerism, and sex. That is the opposite of incarnation, which transforms every I into a sacrament of God. The metanarrative of The Presence is not a cultural grid or national flag to be draped over every people group, but a spiritual DNA that embeds and embodies itself in every tribe and time.[37]

Once again, this part of the Christian metanarrative is a continuation of its parent. God chose the Jews, not to single them out for their superiority, but to anoint them to serve as priests whose parish is the whole world. In the words of Isaiah, whose original insight was to see God already at work in all cultures, even among the enemies of Israel,[38] "I will also make You a light of the nations so that My salvation may reach to the end of the earth."[39] In fact, the Hebrews were originally not a people group at all. Abraham was from an Assyrian or a barbarian culture. God formed Israel out of diverse people groups.

It is enormously significant that Jesus did not make Jerusalem, or the center of Jerusalem, his headquarters. He first based his ministry in Galilee of the Gentiles. His first miracle was in Cana of Galilee; his first sermon was in Nazareth.[40] To be sure, Jesus did not leave Jerusalem behind. He told his disciples to be witnesses "both" in Jerusalem and beyond. But he also didn't tell them to get it "right" in Jerusalem first and then move on to the ends of the earth.[41] Jesus called his disciples to be a "light for revelation to the Gentiles."[42] The word *Gentiles* was a catch-all phrase for every people group other than Jews. "I have set you to be a light for the Gentiles," Jesus said, "that you may bring salvation to the ends of the earth."[43]

Maran-atha leads to Mara-natha. In our Maran-atha role as "incarnants" we are participants in the promised "Mara-natha." The rapture (not rupture) of The Presence leads to Rapture. We can hasten the day[44] of Christ's appearing through our rapture role in body-building—helping the body of Christ reach its full stature by knitting together an indigenized gospel from "every tribe and language and people and nation." [45]

> This gospel of the kingdom will be preached
> in the whole world as a testimony to all nations,
> and then the end will come.
>
> —JESUS[46]

My two favorite images for this double eschatology where the body of Christ both descends and ascends, meeting in the air to form one body, come from artists. One artist is Vincent van Gogh in his famous painting "Starry Night"; the other artist is John of Patmos in his masterpiece "Revelation of Saint John." Van Gogh explained his vision of life after death that lay behind "Starry Night" in words that compared taking a train to reach Spain with taking a terminal illness to reach a star:

Looking at the stars always makes me dream, as simply as I dream over the black dots representing towns and villages on a map. Why, I ask myself, shouldn't the shining dots of the sky be as accessible as the black dots on the map of France? Just as we take the train to get to

Tarascon or Rouen, we take death to reach a star. One thing undoubtedly true in this reasoning is that we cannot get to a star while we are alive, any more than we can take the train when we are dead. So it seems possible to me that cholera, gravel, tuberculosis, and cancer are the celestial means of locomotion, just as steamboats, buses, and railways are terrestrial means. To die quietly of old age would be to go there on foot.[47]

If you look carefully at "Starry Night," you see a double rapture: a form that comes down from above and a form that rises up from the earth, both joining together to become a new star.

The second version of this double rapture is John's vision of the New Jerusalem, as described by biblical scholar Thomas Schmidt. His words cannot be improved or forgotten and deserve more than a footnote in every Manifold Manifesto:

> If we were to create an "artist's reconstruction" [of
> heaven] based on the text of Revelation, the result
> would be far removed from the family reunion in a
> park that most of us long for. Instead, we would see a
> jewel-encrusted, cube-shaped city, fifteen hundred miles
> on a side, called the New Jerusalem. But the precious
> metals and jewels, the mind-boggling and precise dimen-
> sions measured in multiples of twelve, are not intended
> for future generations of illustrators. Rather, the whole
> description signifies unity, community, and order

brought by God out of the botched job people have
made of culture. The idea is not to describe a place but
to depict humanity redeemed. In other words, the New
Jerusalem is a depiction of people as place, not a place for
people.

The fantastic nature of this symbolism may be
strange to a modern audience, but the point is profound
and wonderful. God does not undo civilization or culture
in the end by sending us back, each to a separate garden.
Instead, God *completes* culture by bringing us together in
a perfect "city" characterized by purity and order and harmony and peace. These are of course the very things we
now escape cities to seek. But we can't escape ourselves,
we can't get back to the garden, and we take our chaos
with us everywhere.[48]

NOTES

ACKNOWLEDGMENTS

1. 2 Corinthians 5:14, WEB.
2. This analogy, of course, comes from Acts 9:27 and Exodus 27:8–13.

INTRODUCTION

1. Genesis 3:9.
2. Genesis 4:9.
3. Zygmunt Bauman, *Liquid Love: On the Frailty of Human Bonds* (Malden, MA: Blackwell, 2003), 78.
4. See Daniel 6:10.
5. See Exodus 26:33.
6. See Genesis 18:1–2.
7. See Jonah 1:17.
8. Lorraine Kisly, *The Prayer of Fire: Experiencing the Lord's Prayer* (Brewster, MA: Paraclete, 2004), 39–40. "Throughout the prayer we are asking God to act. In grammatical terms, the phrase is in a tense that demands an action be done now, at this moment, once and for all, and asks for this with urgency." Used by permission of Paraclete Press, www. paracletepress.com.

9. Quoted in Eugene E. Lemcio, "Pirke 'Abot 1:2 (3) and the Synoptic Redactions of the Commands to Love God and Neighbor," *Asbury Theological Journal* 43 (Spring 1988): 46.

10. Proverb quoted by William Vermeulen, "Quotes and Facts #1," *Current Thoughts and Trends,* October 1994, 18.

11. This statistic comes from *Insight on the News,* 11 July 1994, 23. For the population number of 295,734,134, see *The World Factbook–Rank Order–Population,* 9 August 2005, http://www .cia.gov/cia/publications/factbook/rankorder/2119rank.html (accessed 2 September 2005).

12. Robert Strand, *365 Fascinating Facts about Jesus* (Green Forest, AR: New Leaf, 2000), #314.

13. Robert D. Dale, *Seeds for the Future: Growing Organic Leaders for Living Churches* (St. Louis, MO: Lake Hickory Resources, 2005), 11.

14. Henry David Thoreau, *Walden* (Boston: Houghton Mifflin, 1882), 152.

15. Acts 26:9, NEB.

16. See Genesis 6:3 and Deuteronomy 34:7.

17. Elizabeth A. Dreyer brings together these two quotes from Rolheiser and Brueggemann in "Jesus as Bridegroom and Lover: Critical Retrieval of a Medieval Metaphor," *Who Do You Say That I Am? Confessing the Mystery of Christ,* ed. John C. Cavadini and Laura Holt (Notre Dame, IN: University of Notre Dame Press, 2004), 224.

CHAPTER ONE

The epigraph for this chapter is quoted from Bernardo Olivera, "Maturity and Generation: The Spirituality of Our Young People," *Spiritus: A Journal of Christian Spirituality* 3 (Spring 2003): 44, 38–51.

1. William Van Dusen Wishard calls it in his book "Between two ages" [*Between Two Ages: The 21st Century and the Crisis of Meaning* (U.S.A.: XLibris, 2000; rev. ed. 2003)]. I called it almost a decade ago "SoulTsunami" in *SoulTsunami: Sink or Swim in New Millennium Culture* (Grand Rapids, MI: Zondervan, 1999), and before that, "FaithQuakes" in *FaithQuakes* (Nashville: Abingdon, 1994).

2. Philip Larkin, "Annus Mirabilis," *Collected Poems,* ed. Anthony Thwaite (New York: Farrar, Straus, and Giroux, 1989), 167. I have chosen 1962 as the defining year. See Leonard Sweet, *Carpe Mañana: Is Your Church Ready to Seize Tomorrow?* (Grand Rapids, MI: Zondervan, 2001), 14.

3. John McWhorter, *Doing Our Own Thing: The Degradation of Language and Music and Why We Should, Like, Care* (New York: Gotham, 2004), 183. McWhorter names the year 1965 as the pivotal moment in the triumph of pop culture and the pedestrian (which he despises).

4. "An Interview with Margaret Avison," *Image: A Journal of Arts and Religion* 45 (Spring 2005): 76.

5. William Van Dusan Wishard, president of WorldTrends Research, "Understanding Our Moment in History: Living

Between Two Ages," *Vital Speeches of the Day* 71 (1 May 2005), 442.

6. "We are currently living through one of the transforming moments in the history of religion worldwide." So argues Philip Jenkins, *The Next Christendom: The Coming of Global Christianity* (New York: Oxford University Press, 2002), 1. For the significance of the word *re-orienting*, see Leonard Sweet, *Out of the Question...Into the Mystery: Getting Lost in the GodLife Relationship* (Colorado Springs, CO: WaterBrook, 2004), 8–10.

7. Rachel Zoll, "Religion: Evangelical Faiths, Mormon Church Grow Rapidly; Survey: Membership of Liberal Protestant Denominations Declined in the Past Decade, National Study Finds," *Los Angeles Times,* 21 September 2002, B21. Between 1992 and 2002, the Presbyterian Church (USA) lost 11.6 percent of its membership, second only to the United Church of Christ, which lost 14.8 percent of its membership.

8. William Jefferson Clinton, "The Struggle for the Soul of the Twenty-First Century," *NPQ: New Perspectives Quarterly* 19 (Spring 2002): 30.

9. David Sheff, *China Dawn: The Story of a Technology and Business Revolution* (New York: HarperBusiness, 2002), 263.

10. Steve Rosenbush, Catherine Yang, Ronald Grover, Moon Ihlwan, Andy Reinhardt, "Broadband: What's the Holdup?" *Business Week,* 1 March 2004, 38–39.

11. Louise Witt, "2004: A Year of Portentous Change," *American Demographics* 25 (December 2003): 38.

12. John Fetto and Rebecca Gardyn, "You *CAN* Take It with You," *American Demographics,* February 2002, 10. "Of those who work away from the conventional office, the vast majority say they are highly satisfied with their jobs, more productive and exceptionally loyal to their employer, according to an AT&T sponsored survey released in October 2001 by the International Telework Association and Council (ITAC)."

13. Goran Therborn, *Between Sex and Power: Family in the World 1900–2000* (New York: Routledge, 2004), 166. These figures for 1960 and 2000 represent the highest and the lowest percentages for the twentieth century.

14. John Vaughn (jv@churchgrowthtoday.com, www.churchgrowth today.com), founder of Church Growth Today and the Megachurch Research Center, Bolivar, Missouri, quoted in "Black Megachurches' Mega-Outreach," ReligionLink: Resources for Reporters, 8 September 2004, http://www.religion link.org/tip_040908b.php (accessed 2 August 2005).

15. Eudora Welty, "Place in Fiction," *Welty: Stories, Essays and Memoir,* ed. Richard Ford and Michael Kreyling (New York: Literary Classics, 1998), 792.

16. I thank George Wilkie for this distinction between "join" and "join in" in his *Twelve Fragments: Thoughts for Today's Christian* (Edinburgh: Scottish Christian Press, 2005), 25.

17. Gordon William Prange, *At Dawn We Slept: The Untold Story of Pearl Harbor* (New York: McGraw-Hill, 1981).

18. Anthony Thwaite, "Archaeology," *A Move in the Weather: Poems 1994–2002* (London: Enitharmon, 2003), 18.

19. For more on our rampant polytheism, see Nicholas Lash, *Holiness, Speech and Silence: Reflections on the Question of God* (Burlington, VT: Ashgate, 2004), 10.

20. "The crises of globalization…are crises…brought on by the loss of social control over the economy and the weakening of political power in the face of cresohedonic power. In this union of Croesus (money) and Hedone (pleasure) global culture becomes a fashion show, a giant screen, a stereophonic boom, an existence made of glossy, four-color paper. It transforms us into what C. Wright Mills called 'cheerful robots.'" Carlos Fuentes, *This I Believe: An A to Z of a Life* (New York: Random House, 2005), 112.

21. The two dominant forms of "power" today are wealth and fame.

22. Michael McClure, "The Beard," *Evergreen Review Reader, 1967–1973,* ed. Barney Rosset (New York: Four Walls Eight Windows, 1998), 52.

23. It is true that the postmodern tendency to view the "scientific method" as suspiciously as it views any other worldview has given encouragement to what Dick Taverne calls *The March of Unreason: Science, Democracy and the New Fundamentalism* (New York: Oxford University Press, 2005).

24. I love how Robert Dale uses this media phrase "already in progress" as a chapter title in his book *Seeds for the Future: Growing Organic Leaders for Living Churches* (St. Louis, MO: Lake Hickory Resources, November 2005).

25. Deuteronomy 32:7, KJV.

26. From Doris Betts's 2004 E. M. Adams lecture "The Durable Hunger" at the University of North Carolina, in *Image: A Journal of Arts and Religion* 45 (Spring 2005): 95.

CHAPTER TWO

The epigraph for this chapter is taken from *Einstein Quotes,* http://www.heartquotes.net/Einstein.html (accessed 11 August 2005). Alice Calaprice, ed., *The Expanded Quotable Einstein* (Princeton, NJ: Princeton University Press, 2000), 318, indicates this quote attributed to Einstein is probably not by Einstein.

1. From the G. W. Little Lifestyles for the Little Dog catalog http://www.gwlittle.com/search.php?sniff=Fashion%20Club (accessed 7 April 2005).

2. Kevin Liles, quoted in Jason Ankeny, "Falling on Def Ears," Wireless Review, 1 October 2004, http://wirelessreview .com/mag/wireless_falling_def_ears/ (accessed 7 April 2005).

3. Bellagio Hotel and Casino—Communications, "Award Winning Spa and Salon Reopens with New Design and Treatments," press release, Las Vegas, Nevada, 20 December 2002, http://www.bellagio.com/pages/about_press_pressrelease.asp? PressID=104 (accessed 4 August 2005).

4. James Gustave Speth, *Red Sky at Morning: America and the Crisis of the Global Environment* (New Haven, CT: Yale University Press, 2004), 125. I remember Tom Bandy making the same point.

5. Some medical professionals now attribute the increasing number of psychological and physical disorders afflicting people not to viruses or to pollutants, but to our toxic lifestyle, which has become hazardous to our health.

6. Jeremy Cherfas, *The Hunting of the Whale: A Tragedy that Must End* (London: Penguin, 1981), 11.

7. I learned this from Doris Betts, "The Durable Hunger," *Image: A Journal of Arts and Religion* 45 (Spring 2005): 97.

8. 1 Corinthians 15:58.

9. The phrase is derived from John Gillespie Magee Jr. (1922–1941), "High Flight," which begins "Oh! I have slipped the surly bonds of earth." Quoted in *Pilot Officer John G. Magee Jr.—US Air Force Museum—Pre-WWII History Collection,* http://www.wpafb.af.mil/museum/history/prewwii/jgm.htm (accessed 2 September 2005). Also quoted in Dave English, *Slipping the Surly Bonds: Great Quotations on Flight* (New York: McGraw Hill, 1998), 2.

10. Quoted in Siddhartha Deb, "A House Without a Doorstep," *TLS: Times Literary Supplement,* 15 April 2005, 19.

11. For someone else who is asking the same question, see Nicholas Lash, *Holiness, Speech and Silence: Reflections on the Question of God* (Burlington, VT: Ashgate, 2004), 9.

12. The words are from Rushdie's novel, *The Ground Beneath Her Feet* (New York: Henry Holt, 1999), and the melody is by Bono. Salman Rushdie, *Step Across This Line: Collected Nonfiction 1992–2002* (New York: Random House, 2002), 96.

13. See his recent book of essays, *Step Across This Line: Collected Nonfiction 1992–2002* (New York: Random House, 2002). Also see his interview by Shikha Dalmia, "The Iconoclast," *Reason,* August 2005, 23–28.

14. See Christopher Booker, *The Seven Basic Plots: Why We Tell Stories* (New York: Continuum, 2005), who argues that there are only seven plots: Overcoming the monster, rags to riches, the quest, voyage and return, comedy, tragedy, and rebirth (21–213). He admits two other plot types: "Rebellion Against the One (for example, *1984* and *Brave New World* [495–503]) and Mystery (one of the most popular forms of storytelling in the modern world) [505–15])."

15. Lash, *Holiness, Speech and Silence,* 29. For Lash, "the Christian story of everything" is "the story of God's being a gift, as self-gift establishing and enlivening the world" (43).

16. Lash, *Holiness, Speech and Silence,* 31.

17. Jacques Dupuis, *Toward a Christian Theology of Religious Pluralism* (Maryknoll, NY: Orbis, 1997), 299.

18. Adin Steinsaltz, *On Being Free,* ed. Arthur Kurzweil (Northvale, NJ: Jason Aronson, 1995), 194.

19. For an excellent introduction to the topic of globalization, see David Held and Anthony McGrew, "The Great Globalization Debate: An Introduction," *The Global Transformations Reader: An Introduction to the Globalization Debate* (Malden, MA: Polity, 2000), 1–45.

20. Roland Robertson calls USAmerican churches "globophobic," as referenced in Tim Dearborn, "A Global Future for Local

Churches," *The Local Church in a Global Era: Reflections for a New Century*, ed. Max L. Stackhouse, Tim Dearborn, and Scott Paeth (Grand Rapids, MI: Eerdmans, 2000), 209.

21. Pierre Teilhard de Chardin, *Activation of Energy* (New York: Harcourt Brace Jovanovich, 1970), 239. With thanks to John F. Haught, distinguished research professor at Georgetown University, for this reference.

22. Ephesians 1:18.

23. See for example, Romans 1:15, TNIV: "I am so eager to preach the gospel also to you who are in Rome."

24. Acts 9:6.

25. Tom Paulin, "Nostalgia for the Future?" *The Invasion Handbook* (London: Faber and Faber, 2002), 133.

26. Miroslav Volf, "Love's Memory: The Role of Memory in Contemporary Culture," Princeton Theological Seminary Institute for Youth Ministry, 2002, 61, http://www.ptsem.edu/iym/research/lectures/downloads/2002/1volf.pdf (accessed 17 January 2005).

27. Quoted in Hal Niedzviecki, *Hello, I'm Special: How Individuality Became the New Conformity* (Toronto: Penguin Canada, 2004), 147–48.

28. Matthew 18:10, TNIV.

29. Reminiscent of Rodin's *The Thinker*.

30. Thomas E. Schmidt, *A Scandalous Beauty: The Artistry of God and the Way of the Cross* (Grand Rapids, MI: Brazos, 2002), 8.

31. Calaprice, *The Expanded Quotable Einstein*, 319, indicates that this quote attributed to Einstein is probably not by Einstein.

32. Wendell Berry, *Life Is a Miracle: An Essay Against Modern Superstition* (Washington DC: Counterpoint, 2000), 45.

33. Acts 17:30.

34. John 3:16.

35. Psalm 91, NKJV.

CHAPTER THREE

1. Luke 11:2.

2. Bruce Chilton, "Regnum Dei Deus Est," *Scottish Journal of Theology* 31 (1978): 261, 267, 270. See also Bruce Chilton, *Pure Kingdom: Jesus' Vision of God* (Grand Rapids, MI: Eerdmans, 1996), ix, 11–15.

3. Luke 16:16.

4. This is one of the insights of the excellent article by Bernard Hamilton on the "puzzling success" of *The Da Vinci Code*, "Puzzling Success," *TLS: Times Literary Supplement*, 10 June 2005, 20–21.

5. Umberto Eco, *Foucault's Pendulum*, trans. William Weaver (San Diego, CA: Harcourt Brace Jovanovich, 1988), 620.

6. Matthew 6:33.

7. Matthew 6:10.

8. John 6:15.

9. Luke 12:32.

10. Matthew 4:17—"The kingdom of heaven has come near"; Luke 10:9—"The kingdom of God has come near to you"; Mark 12:34—"You are not far from the kingdom of God."

11. For more on this "heavily fortified kingdom of self" see Rick Barger, *A New and Right Spirit: Creating an Authentic Church in a Consumer Culture* (Herndon, VA: Alban Institute, 2005), 22.

12. Quoted in P. J. Kavanagh, "Bywords," *TLS: Times Literary Supplement,* 4 June 1999, 16.

13. Hillel Zeitlin: "In many religions there is the notion of a book or doctrine that comes from heaven. We Jews, however, believe that the Torah itself is heaven." Quoted in Adin Steinsaltz, *On Being Free,* ed. Arthur Kurzweil (Northvale, NJ: Jason Aronson, 1995), 192.

14. Matthew 28:20, NASB.

15. John 14:6, NASB.

16. Luke 17:20–21.

17. See 2 Thessalonians 1:9.

18. Deuteronomy 30:12–14.

19. Psalm 91:1, MSG.

20. Psalm 16:11.

21. William Blake, "On Another's Sorrow," *The Poetical Works of William Blake,* ed. John Sampson (London: Oxford University Press, 1913), 78.

22. Joel S. Goldsmith, *Practicing the Presence* (London: Fowler, 1958), 9–10.

23. See for example Goldsmith, *Practicing the Presence,* 12–17. See also David R. Mains, ed., *The Bible for Personal Revival: Practicing the Presence of Jesus* (Grand Rapids, MI: Zondervan, 1998);

Mike Mason, *Practicing the Presence of People: How We Learn to Love* (Colorado Springs, CO: WaterBrook, 1999); Kerry S. Walters, *Practicing Presence: The Spirituality of Caring in Everyday Life* (Franklin, WI: Sheed and Ward, 2001); and—I love this title—Deborah G. Whitehouse and C. Alan Anderson, *Practicing the Presence of God for Practical Purposes* (Bloomington, IN: 1st Books, 2000).

24. 2 Corinthians 4:10.

25. John 15:7.

26. 1 Peter 1:23, NKJV.

27. 1 John 2:14.

28. With thanks to John Knipper, "How to Say 'I Love You' in Different Languages," http://www.galactic-guide.com/articles/2R95.html (accessed 7 April 2005).

CHAPTER FOUR

1. Jack Paar, *P. S. Jack Paar* (Garden City, NY: Doubleday, 1983), 22, quoted in Leonard Sweet, "The Monsters We're All Afraid Of," *PreachingPlus,* 28 October 2001.

2. Some of the best training I received as a historian was not to use the first person singular in writing. Despite all the talk about community, the "I" is omnipresent in the literature of spirituality and even that of the emerging church.

3. Joel S. Goldsmith, *Practicing the Presence* (London: Fowler, 1958), 54–55.

4. Quoted in Carlos Fuentes, *This I Believe: An A to Z of a Life* (New York: Random House, 2005), 303.

5. Richard Sennett, *The Corrosion of Character: The Personal Consequences of Work in the New Capitalism* (New York: Norton, 1998), 136–48.

6. For variant translations, see Ludwig Wittgenstein, *Culture and Value,* ed. G. H. von Wright and Heikki Nyman, trans. Peter Winch (Chicago: University of Chicago Press, 1984), 45e, 46e.

7. In the USAmerican Civil War, Union dead were often interred in individual graves, while Confederate soldiers were mostly mass graved. At Shiloh there are more than five mass graves containing the remains of Confederate casualties. But the tradition of individual graves was not standard until after the First World War.

8. Gregory H. Hemingway, *Papa: A Personal Memoir* (Boston: Houghton Mifflin, 1976), 93.

9. Lynn Revell, "The Return of the Sacred," *Marxism, Mysticism and Modern Theory,* ed. Suke Wolton (London: Macmillan, 1996), 130.

10. Ken Blanchard and Phil Hodges, *The Servant Leader: Transforming Your Heart, Head, Hands, and Habits* (Nashville: J. Countryman, 2003), 26.

11. Euclid O. Smith cites this stunning statistic in *When Culture and Biology Collide: Why We Are Stressed, Depressed and Self-Obsessed* (New Brunswick, NJ: Rutgers University Press, 2002), 93.

12. Have you seen the photographs of dogs that resemble their owners? It's true. We even choose "all about me" dogs—pets that resemble us. Some say this is because we trust those who look something like us because it indicates genetic relatedness and you can trust "relatives" more than strangers. For more on this, see Christina Payne and Klaus Jaffe, "Self Seeks Like: Many Humans Choose Their Dog-Pets Following Rules Used for Assortive Mating," *Journal of Ethnology* 23 (2005): 15–18, http://atta.labb.usb.ve/Klaus/Dog%20pet%20selection.pdf (accessed 13 April 2005), 2.

13. David Shibley, *The Missions Addiction: Capturing God's Passion for the World* (Lake Mary, FL: Charisma House, 2001), 30.

14. Austin Farrer, "Grace and Resurrection," *Austin Farrer: The Essential Sermons,* ed. Leslie Houlden (Cambridge, MA: Cowley, 1991), 137.

15. Pope John Paul II, "General Audience, Wednesday, 9 September 1998," http://www.vatican.va/holy_father/john_paul_ii/audiences/1998/documents/hf_jp-ii_aud_09091998_en.html (accessed 20 September 2005).

16. A version of this anonymous prayer even appears in "York Community Church Prayers," York, England, http://www.yorkcommunitychurch.co.uk/prayers.html (accessed 4 August 2005). If any reader can confirm the original source of this prayer, please send it to WaterBrook Press, 12265 Oracle Boulevard, Suite 200, Colorado Springs, Colorado 80921, and we will include the attribution in a later printing of this book.

17. Compare Anne Lamott's "two best prayers" she says daily: "Help me, help me, help me" and "Thank you, thank you, thank you," in *Traveling Mercies: Some Thoughts on Faith* (New York: Pantheon, 1999), 82, and a third prayer, "Wow!" which Lamott added later and is quoted in John M. Buchanan's sermon, "Reverence," 8 February 2004, Fourth Presbyterian Church, Chicago, Illinois, http://www.fourthchurch.org/020804sermon.html (accessed 8 August 2005).

18. Louis Jacobs, "Ethics 2," *Jewish Preaching: Homilies and Sermons* (Portland, OR: Vallentine Mitchell, 2004), 217.

19. In the words of Mexican novelist Carlos Fuentes, written shortly before his death in 1999: "Perhaps 'I' is not the most honorable pronoun. But there is no 'you' that does not come from or direct itself toward the 'I,' nor is there a 'you' and 'I' that can be extricable from the 'we.' Yet at the same time, can there be a 'we' that expels the 'I' and the 'you' from its dangerous community without also becoming a perilous political abstraction." *This I Believe: An A to Z of a Life* (New York: Random House, 2005), 304.

20. Mishnah (Sanhedrin 4:5b). See for example, *Tractate Sanhedrin: Mishnah and Tosefta: The Judicial Procedure of the Jews as Codified towards the End of the Second Century A.D.*, trans. Herbert Danby (New York: Macmillan, 1919), 79.

21. See Zygmunt Bauman's foreword to Ulrich Beck and Elisabeth Beck-Gernsheim, *Individualization: Institutionalized Individualism and Its Social and Political Consequences* (Thousand Oaks, CA: Sage, 2002), xv.

22. I first encountered this phrase in Paul Leinberger and Bruce Tucker, *The New Individualists: The Generation After "The Organization Man"* (New York: HarperCollins, 1991), 232–33.

23. John Brewer, "Ego in the Arcades," *TLS: Times Literary Supplement,* 22 October 2004), 3–4.

24. Creating our own identity puts us "on our own" in more ways than one. The modern world had all the connectedness of an Edward Hopper interior, isolated and withdrawn, with one in three of us admitting to never having spent an evening with a neighbor. Our social malnutrition helps explain why twenty-five million USAmericans will participate in the oxymoronic phenomenon of "self-help groups" at some time during the course of their lives. (If we get into a mess all by ourselves, how can we hope to get back out through self-help?) Study conducted by researchers at the University of Texas at Austin, and reported in John Fetto, "Lean on Me: Use of Self-Help Groups" *American Demographics,* December 2000, 16, http://demographics.com/ (accessed 26 January 2001).

25. This is, of course, a rewrite of Andy Warhol's adage that in the future everyone will have their fifteen minutes of fame. Quoted in Hal Niedzviecki, *Hello, I'm Special: How Individuality Became The New Conformity* (Toronto: Penguin Canada, 2004), 27.

26. Strategies for stealing your identity range from low tech (lost mail or stolen mail, shoulder surfing, dumpster diving) to high tech (phishing, pharming, keylogging, social engineering). But no matter what method is employed, identity theft is one of the

worst nightmares of your life, resulting in financial loss, a bad credit rating, and untold hours of phone calls undoing the damage.

27. Benedict Carey, "Who's Mentally Ill? Deciding Is Often All in the Mind," *New York Times*, 12 June 2005, Sec. 4, 16.

28. Fuentes, *This I Believe*, 44.

29. Acquiescing to a prefabricated I brings to the fore various "identity issues" and necessitates constant "identity checks," which the culture is happy to provide (for a price, of course). Canadian novelist and fiction editor Hal Niedzviecki describes this phenomenon well: "In the absence of any uniqueness test or other definitive way to ascertain how special the person standing next to us might be, most of us turn to pre-established signs and symbols that can project a sense of our own individuality. Essentially, in our ongoing bid to demonstrate that we are special individuals, we require an endless supply of limited-edition, handmade, one-time-only products, contests, and events capable of conveying at least some partial sense of our uniqueness to everyone from co-workers and friends to people we pass on the street." *Hello, I'm Special*, 19.

Along these same lines, Stanley Kubrick's last film was titled *Eyes Wide Shut*. In the opening scene between the physician husband and wife, we hear these two questions: "Honey, have you seen my wallet?" and "How do I look?" *Eyes Wide Shut* [videorecording], screenplay by Stanley Kubrick and Frederick Raphael (Burbank, CA: Warner Home Video, 1999).

30. This is the author's paraphrase of 1 Corinthians 3:16: "Do you not know that you are God's temple?"

31. In her defense of choices that "maximize" and not merely "satisfice," cultural critic Virginia Postrel argues: "The more freedom we have to control our lives, the more responsibility we have for how they turn out. In a world of constraints, learning to be happy with what you're given is a virtue. In a world of choices, virtue comes from learning to make commitments without regrets. And commitment, in turn, requires self-confidence and self-knowledge." "Consumer Vertigo," *Reason,* June 2005, 54.

32. Kwame Anthony Appiah, *The Ethics of Identity* (Princeton, NJ: Princeton University Press, 2005), 35.

33. Needless to say, this only works in English.

34. Cf. Galatians 2:20, KJV.

35. See Matthew 10:29, 31; Luke 12:6.

36. Mark 3:33, cf. Matthew 12:48.

37. Luke 9:62.

38. Luke 9:60.

39. Matthew 10:35.

40. Luke 12:49.

41. Edwin Friedman, "Leadership Through Self-Differentiation, A Series of Talks Presented by the Seven Oaks Foundation," *Dr. Friedman Speaks,* audiocassette (Silver Spring, MD: Seven Oaks Foundation, 1980–1989), transcription available online at Family Systems II, http://www.clt.astate.edu/dwcox/family_systems_ii.htm (accessed 11 August 2005).

42. Everyone needs a discrete sense of self, and without this cummerbund of consciousness we bleed to death. Russian novelist Vladimir Nabokov made "discreteness" into a constituent characteristic of life itself: "Unless a film of flesh envelops us, we die. Man exists only insofar as he is separated from his surroundings. The cranium is a space-traveler's helmet. Stay inside or you perish. Death is divestment, death is communion. It may be wonderful to mix with the landscape, but to do so is the end of the tender ego." Quoted by C. D. C. Reeve, *Love's Confusions* (Cambridge, MA: Harvard University Press, 2005), 8.

43. Richard Foster, *Prayer: Finding the Heart's True Home,* 159–60. While the thought is based on John Dalrymple's writing, only the secondary quotes are from his *Simple Prayer* (Wilmington, DE: Michael Glazier, 1984), 109–10. See also Leonard Sweet, *Jesus Drives Me Crazy* (Grand Rapids, MI: Zondervan, 2003), 111–12.

44. Søren Kierkegaard, *The Sickness Unto Death: A Christian Psychological Exposition for Upbuilding and Awakening,* ed. Howard V. Hong and Edna H. Hong (Princeton, NJ: Princeton University Press, 1980), 30.

45. Sociologist at the London School of Economics, David Martin, "Loss and Realization of Life," *Christian Language in the Secular City* (Burlington, VT: Ashgate, 2002), 91.

46. Frank Furedi, *Therapy Culture: Cultivating Vulnerability in an Uncertain Age* (New York: Routledge, 2004), 153. The quote from Professor Nicholas Emler of the London School of Economics is found on page 158.

47. Erich Fromm was one of the first to point this out long ago in *To Have Or To Be?* (New York: Harper and Row, 1976), 21.

48. The first psychiatric diagnostic manual was published in 1952 and included sixty disorders. There are now three hundred disorders listed and defined. They include kleptomania to hyposomnia (oversleeping) to borderline personality disorder. See Carey, "Who's Mentally Ill?" Psychologists at the University of Leicester have identified celebrity worship syndrome (CWS), an obsessive addictive behavior that affects one in three people to some degree and may become a "serious clinical issue." For more on this, see John Maltby, James Houran, and Lynn E. McCutcheon, "A Clinical Interpretation of Attitudes and Behaviors Associated with Celebrity Worship," *Journal of Nervous and Mental Disease* 191 (January 2003): 25–29.

49. Ingmar Bergman condemned the current preoccupation with the self among artists and film-makers in precisely these terms for precisely this reason: "Today the individual has become the highest form and the greatest bane of artistic creation. The smallest wound or pain of the ego is examined under a microscope as if it were of eternal importance. The artist considers his isolation, his subjectivity, his individualism almost holy. Thus we finally gather in one large pen, where we stand and bleat about our loneliness without listening to each other and without realizing that we are smothering each other to death. The individualists stare into each other's eyes and yet deny the existence of each other. We walk in circles, so limited by our own anxieties that we can no longer distinguish between true and

false, between the gangster's whim and the purest ideal." Quoted by artist/engraver Barry Moser in "Redeeming the Time: A Symposium," *Image: Journal of the Arts and Religion* 42 (Spring/Summer 2004): 78.

50. Furedi, *Therapy Culture,* 153.

51. Alison Elliot, *The Miraculous Everyday* (Edinburgh: Covenanters, 2005), 28. Used by permission.

52. For this approach see Christina Hoff Sommers and Sally Satel, *One Nation Under Therapy: How the Helping Culture Is Eroding Self-Reliance* (New York: St. Martin's Press, 2005). In this book the authors coin the word "therapism" to describe our tendency to "valorize openness, emotional self-absorption and the sharings of feelings" (5). They call for an emotional temperance movement and a return to self-reliance, which unfortunately is but another form of self-obsession.

53. Joann Wolski Conn, *Women's Spirituality: Resources for Christian Development* (New York: Paulist, 1986), 3.

54. Thomas Moore, "Will We Take the Moral Values Challenge?" *Spirituality and Health: The Soul/Body Connection,* January/February 2005, http://www.spiritualityhealth.com/newsh/items/article/item_9574.html (accessed 8 April 2005).

55. Isaiah 53:6.

56. Howard Gardner's view is, "The whole course of human development can be viewed as a continuing decline in egocentrism." *Quest for Mind: Piaget, Lévi Strauss, and the Structuralist Movement,* 2d ed. (Chicago: University of Chicago Press, 1981), 63.

57. For more on what makes the American success story such a "bro-

ken" story, see Daniel Taylor, *Tell Me a Story: The Life-Shaping Power of Our Stories* (St. Paul, MN: Bog Walk, 2001), 130.

58. Each step is a chapter heading in Rick Pitino with Bill Reynolds, *Success Is a Choice: Ten Steps to Overachieving in Business and Life* (New York: Broadway, 1997).

59. Leviticus 14:4, KJV. This was the one for infectious skin diseases, including leprosy.

60. Louis Jacobs, "Metzora," *Jewish Preaching: Homilies and Sermons* (Portland, OR: Vallentine Mitchell, 2004), 118.

61. The following words of advice were given to his son from the Jewish rabbi/philosopher Nahmanides (1194–1270): "If the man you meet is clearly your better in learning, in character, or in achievement, there is no room for pride. But even if you are superior to him in these things, reflect that your responsibilities are thereby the greater. God has been more lavish in His gifts to you and more is demanded of you." Quoted in Jacobs, "Metzora," *Jewish Preaching*, 118.

62. With apologies to Yale Professor Harold J. Morowitz for mangling his categories. *Ego Niches: An Ecological View of Organizational Behavior* (Woodbridge, CT: Ox Bow, 1977), 30–84.

63. Arthur O. Roberts, *The Atonement*, http://www.quakerinfo.com/atonement.shtml (accessed 7 April 2005).

64. The second and fourth stanzas of Luther B. Bridgers's 1910 hymn "He Keeps Me Singing," *Hymns of Praise Numbers One and Two Combined for the Church and Sunday School*, comp. F. G. Kingsbury (Chicago: Hope Publishing, 1926), 363. The story behind the hymn can be found in William Jensen

Reynolds, *Hymns of Our Faith: A Handbook for the Baptist Hymnal* (Nashville: Broadman, 1964), 210, 258–59.

65. Psalm 23:6.

66. Psalm 27:4 (NKJV), which states, "Your face, LORD, I will seek," is the theme verse for John Updike's 2003 novel *Seek My Face*. I am still trying to figure out what it means (if anything) that both Updike's first novel (*Poorhouse Fair* [Greenwich, Conn.: Fawcett, 1958]) and his twentieth (*Seek My Face* [New York: Alfred A. Knopf, 2002]) take place over the course of one day.

67. Psalm 27:4, 8–9, TNIV.

68. Brian Volck, "A Conversation with Gil Bailie," *Image: A Journal of Arts and Religion* 41 (Winter 2003): 63–77, 71.

69. When featured on the cover of *Esquire*'s "heroes" edition, quoted in Fred Rogers, *You are Special: Words of Wisdom from America's Most Beloved Neighbor* (New York: Viking, 1994), 115.

70. Volck, "A Conversation," 71.

71. Volck, "A Conversation," 71.

72. For more on masks and "true colors," see Leonard Sweet, *Jesus Drives Me Crazy* (Grand Rapids, MI: Zondervan, 2003), 41–50.

73. James H. Olthuis, "Crossing the Threshold: Sojourning Together in the Wild Spaces of Love," in Smith and Venema, eds., *Hermeneutics of Charity,* 33.

74. If any reader can provide the source of this quote, please send it to WaterBrook Press, 12265 Oracle Boulevard, Suite 200, Colorado Springs, Colorado 80921, and we will include the attribution in a later printing of this book.

CHAPTER FIVE

The epigraph for this chapter is taken from Teresa of Avila, *Interior Castle*, trans. Kieran Kavanaugh and Otilio Rodriguez (New York: Paulist, 1979), 70, [4.1.7].

1. Gregory McNamee, *Gila: The Life and Death of an American River* (New York: Orion, 1994), 147–48.
2. Black Eyed Peas, "Where Is the Love?" www.lyricsondemand .com/b/blackeyedpeaslyrics/whereisthelovelyrics.html (accessed 21 November 2005).
3. *Saint Thérèse of Lisieux: Her Last Conversations,* ed. and trans. John Clarke (Washington DC: Institute of Carmelite Studies, 1977), 217.
4. Zygmunt Bauman, *Liquid Love: On the Frailty of Human Bonds* (Malden, MA: Blackwell, 2003), viii.
5. This is an adaptation of the story as told in Adin Steinsaltz, *Simple Words: Thinking About What Really Matters in Life,* ed. Elana Schachter and Ditsa Shabtai (New York: Simon and Schuster, 1999), 190–91.
6. So argues Sam Keen. This sentiment is quoted from the movie *Love Story,* as well as from the best-selling novel *Love Story* by Erich Segal (New York: New American Library, 1970), 91, 131. The actual statement made twice in the novel is this: "Love means not ever having to say you're sorry."
7. See Luke 7:47.

8. *Kierkegaard's Concluding Unscientific Postscript,* trans. David F. Swenson and Walter Lowrie (Princeton, NJ: Princeton University Press, 1941), 205.

9. See Luke 10:27 and Deuteronomy 6:5.

10. As reported in the study by the Glenmary Research Center in Nashville, Tennessee, and quoted in Rachel Zoll, "Religion: Evangelical Faiths, Mormon Church Grow Rapidly; Survey: Membership of Liberal Protestant Denominations Declined in the Past Decade, National Study Finds," *Los Angeles Times,* 21 September 2002, B21.

11. John 15:13.

12. Quoted in Church of Scotland's Greyfriars Christmas Day Message, 2004, http://www.churchofscotland.org.uk/serving scotland/downloads/modchristmasspeech04.txt (accessed 3 September 2005).

13. George F. MacLeod, "A Chaos of Uncalculating Love," *The Whole Earth Shall Cry Glory: Iona Prayers* (Isle of Iona: Wild Goose Publications, 1985), 40, www.ionabooks.com. Used by permission.

14. MacLeod, "A Chaos of Uncalculating Love," 40, www .ionabooks.com. Used by permission.

15. See Ephesians 2:21; 1 Corinthians 3:16; 2 Corinthians 6:16.

16. See Exodus 25:21–22.

17. Ephesians 3:18–19.

18. Ephesians 3:19.

19. See Ignacio Ellacuría, "Utopia and Prophecy in Latin America," trans. James Brockman, *Mysterium Liberationis,* ed. Ignacio

Ellacuría and Jon Sobrino (Maryknoll, NY: Orbis, 1993), 315–16, 324.

20. The Greek term is *politeumai*. See Philippians 1:27.

21. Pope John Paul II, "Instruction on Certain Aspects of 'Theology of Liberation,'" to Sacred Congregation for the Doctrine of the Faith, 6 August 1984. *Catholic Library: Instruction on "Theology of Liberation,"* http://www.newadvent.org/library/docs_df84lt.htm (accessed 4 September 2005).

22. Rabbi Chananiah, quoted in *Pirke Aboth: Sayings of the Fathers,* ed. Isaac Unterman (New York: Twayne, 1964), 160.

23. Psalm 101:2.

24. Matthew 18:20.

25. Matthew 28:20.

26. Words spoken by John Nash (Russell Crowe) near the conclusion of the movie *A Beautiful Mind,* directed by Ron Howard (Universal City, CA: Universal Pictures, 2001). See also the screenplay by Akiva Goldsman, *A Beautiful Mind: The Shooting Script* (New York: Newmarket, 2002), 117.

27. James H. Olthuis, *The Beautiful Risk: A New Psychology of Loving and Being Loved* (Grand Rapids, MI: Zondervan, 2001), 71.

28. 1 John 4:19.

29. "In *Beauty and the Beast,* it is only when the Beast discovers that Beauty really loves him in all his ugliness that he himself becomes beautiful." Frederick Buechner, *Wishful Thinking: A Theological ABC* (New York: Harper, 1973), 85.

30. Ellacuría, "Utopia and Prophecy," 312.

31. Anders Nygren, *Kristna Kärlekstanken* (Stockholm: Svenska Kyrkans Diakonistyrelsen, 1930–1936; translated as *Agape and Eros,* trans. Philip S. Watson (Philadelphia, PA: Westminster, 1953), 1: 236.

32. 1 John 4:7–8.

33. 1 John 4:9–10.

34. Attributed to Baal Shem Tov, Ukrainian founder of the Hasidic movement of Judaism.

35. Maya Angelou, *Wouldn't Take Nothing for My Journey Now* (New York: Random House, 1993), 75.

36. Philip P. Bliss, "Jesus Loves Even Me," *Memoirs of Philip P. Bliss,* ed. D. W. Whittle (New York: A. S. Barnes, 1877), 130.

37. 1 Corinthians 13:13.

38. Austin Farrer, "The Country Doctor," *Austin Farrer: The Essential Sermons,* ed. Leslie Houlden (Cambridge, MA: Cowley, 1991), 206.

39. 1 Corinthians 14:1, MSG.

40. James H. Olthuis, "Crossing the Threshold: Sojourning Together in the Wild Spaces of Love," *Hermeneutics of Charity: Interpretation, Selfhood, and Postmodern Faith,* ed. James K. A. Smith and Henry Isaac Venema (Grand Rapids, MI: Brazos, 2004), 38.

41. Isaiah 66:1.

42. Psalm 11:4.

43. These are the first lines of John Agard, "Anancy's Thoughts on Hospitality," *Weblines* (Newcastle upon Tyne: Bloodaxe, 2002), 58. Used by permission.

44. This Fromme quote is from Ron Hutchcraft, *5 Needs Your Child Must Have Met at Home* (Grand Rapids, MI: Zondervan, 1994), 101. For more on the story of her life see Jess Bravin, *Squeaky: The Life and Times of Lynette Alice Fromme* (New York: St. Martin's, 1997), 15–47. An alternative version of "Squeaky" Fromme's explanation for why she followed Manson goes like this: "A dog goes to somebody who loves it and takes care of it." Richard Steele, "The Story of Squeaky," *Newsweek,* 15 September 1975, 18.

45. 1 John 4:7, MSG.

46. "Do you expect a pat on the back?" Luke 6:32, MSG.

47. Ezekiel 36:26, TNIV.

48. From a sermon preached six years before his death and quoted in Grace Adolphsen Brame, *Faith, the Yes of the Heart* (Minneapolis: Augsburg, 1999), 17.

49. Paraphrase of Sirach 17, quoted by Bruno Cortis, MD, "Win with Your Heart Intelligence," http://www.brunocortis.com/win.htm (accessed 20 September 2005). The Jerusalem Bible version states: "The LORD gave human beings 'a heart to think with.... He put his own light in their hearts to show them the magnificence of his works" (17:6/5–8/7).

50. Quoted in *Sowing Seeds of Hope—Beginning World Vision,* http://www.worldvision.org.tw/english/wv1.html (accessed 3 September 2005).

51. John Wesley didn't preach fewer than fifteen sermons a week over the course of his ministry. Of the almost fifty thousand sermons Wesley preached, his personal favorite was called "The

Circumcision of the Heart." The theme was that only love could "circumcise the heart." The promise of The Presence is that out of a heart circumcised by love, God will give us a new heart. For more on Wesley's favorite sermon, see John Wesley, "The Circumcision of the Heart," *The Works of John Wesley,* vol. 1, *Sermons 1–33,* ed. Albert C. Outler (Nashville: Abingdon, 1984), 401–14. For more on John Wesley's sermons, see www.Bibleteacher.org. Classical Biblical Christianity—Sermons in the File Cabinet, http://www.bibleteacher.org/sermons2b.htm (accessed 24 August 2005). According to information at this Web site, Wesley preached an average of eight hundred sermons a year for sixty years. If my math is correct, that would be forty-eight thousand in his lifetime.

52. C. S. Lewis, *The Four Loves* (New York: Harcourt, Brace and World, 1960), 169.

53. To talk about love means also needing to talk about its opposite: evil. To fail in love relationships is the ultimate in evil.

Margie Balter is based in Los Angeles, where she has an unusual business. She gives crash courses to actors in how to bluff their way through Bach, how to pretend to play the piano so it looks like you're really doing it. Actors such as Tom Cruise, Scarlett Johansson, and Sandra Bullock come to Balter for help, and she takes them from "Chopsticks" to Chopin in a few weeks.

Some of these actors get very good at pretending to play difficult music. But Balter says there is one telltale sign that gives away whether you're a rookie or a professional. If you're a real pianist, she comments, "the fingers always stay on the keys."

Love's fingers always stay on the keys. Even when the playing gets hard and the beautiful chords don't come, love stays put. We go the distance in love, not because we see less of the evil that is in the world but because we see more. And seeing everything that is there, we love more.

For more on the story of Margie Balter, see Meline Toumani, "The 60-Day Course in Perfect Fake Piano Playing," *New York Times,* 10 July 2005, 2.1.

54. The annual rituals of the Holy of Holies, during which the high priest had a rope attached to his waist in case he was smitten dead for unworthiness, are well known. Less talked about were the signs warning Gentiles not to proceed any further in the Temple, upon penalty of death (cf. Acts 21:28).

55. In Cleveland, Ohio, the Institute for Research on Unlimited Love (IRUL) encourages scientific research into love and explores the impact on life of deep, nonsuperficial love. What's so amazing about this is that such an institute exists. Science loves to study the impact of negative human behavior. For example, there are more than one hundred thousand peer-reviewed scientific studies on depression, but just seven on happiness.

Here is the institute's definition of "unlimited love": "The essence of love is to affectively affirm as well as to unselfishly delight in the well-being of others, and to engage in acts of care and service on their behalf; unlimited love extends this love to all others without exception, in an enduring and constant way. Widely considered the highest form of virtue, unlimited love is often deemed a Creative Presence underlying and integral to all of reality: participation in unlimited love constitutes the fullest experience of spirituality."

The definition of unlimited love is taken from The Institute for Research on Unlimited Love, Welcome letter, http://www .unlimitedloveinstitute.org/welcome/index.html (accessed 10 April 2005). For more on the scientific study of love, see Kristin Ohlson, "Love Doctors: Scientists Study the Value of Selflessness," *Utne,* January–February 2005, 24–27. See also Elliot Sober and David Sloan Wilson's study of altruism, *Unto Others: The Evolution and Psychology of Unselfish Behavior* (Cambridge: Harvard University Press, 1998), which begins: "Even saints could be regarded as selfish if they perceived their lives of sacrifice as tickets to heaven" (17).

56. "What Wondrous Love Is This," *The Southern Harmony and Musical Companion, Containing a Choice Collection of Tunes, Hymns, Psalms, Odes, and Anthems Selected from the Most Eminent Authors in the United States…*by William Walker, ed. Glenn C. Wilcox (Lexington, Ky.: University Press of Kentucky, 1987; repr. of the 1854 ed.), 252. See also "What Wondrous Love Is This," USAmerican folk hymn, attributed by some to Alexander Means, with music from *The Southern Harmony,* 1835, http://www.cyberhymnal.org/htm/w/h/a/whatwond.htm (accessed 9 April 2005).

57. Daniel Swift, "Chronicle Dating: What's Love Got To Do With It?" *New York Times Book Review,* 03 April 2005, 31.

58. Frank Tallis, *Love Sick: Love as Mental Illness* (New York: Thunder's Mouth, 2005), 60.

59. Tallis, *Love Sick,* 9. Tallis adds that "to be romantically involved is an admission that carries a host of implications: passion, folly, obsession, anguish, recklessness, intrigue, and adventure" (87–88).

60. So say historian Lawrence Stone, sociologist Anthony Giddens, and psychologist Ethel Spector Person. See J. Davis, "Literate Cultures, Oral Asides," *TLS: Times Literary Supplement,* 30 July 1999, 6.

61. Genesis 29:20, TNIV.

62. David Yount, *Celebrating the Rest of Your Life* (Minneapolis: Augsburg, 2005), 136.

63. Mother Teresa, *The Path of Love: Stories,* "Joy and Prayer," http://home.comcast.net/~motherteresasite/stories.html (accessed 11 April 2005).

64. Serge Moscovici, *Society Against Nature: The Emergence of Human Societies* (Atlantic Highlands, NJ: Humanities, 1976), 149.

65. Sociologist Zygmunt Bauman writes movingly of the widening gap between what we are made aware of and what we do anything about. See Zygmunt Bauman, *Liquid Love: On the Frailty of Human Bonds* (Malden, MA: Blackwell, 2003), 97. We have plenty of "tele-vision," Bauman writes, but we have very little "tele-action." See *Liquid Love,* 96.

66. Katharine Craik, "Every Man in His Humour," *TLS: Times Literary Supplement,* 7 January 2005, 23.

67. Canticle 8:6b. For this interpretation of Song of Solomon 8:6, see Roland E. Murphy, "Canticle of Canticles" *The New Jerome Biblical Commentary*, eds., Raymond E. Brown, Joseph A. Fitzmyer, and Roland E. Murphy (Englewood Cliffs, NJ: Prentice-Hall, 1990), 465.

68. It was believed that a house in which a Yule log smoldered could never be struck by lightning. See Christopher Dewdney, *Acquainted with the Night: Excursions Through the World After Dark* (New York: Bloomsbury, 2004), 125–26.

69. Others who have understood *eros* as integral to *agape* include Julian of Norwich and more recently, Jean Vanier of L'Arche communities. Gillian T. W. Ahlgren, "Julian of Norwich's Theology of *Eros*," *Spiritus* 5 (2005), 37–53.

70. Hebrews 12:29.

71. 1 Corinthians 3:15, KJV.

72. Mother Teresa, *The Path of Love: Stories*, "Joy and Prayer."

73. Nicholas Lash, *Holiness, Speech and Silence: Reflections on the Question of God* (Burlington, VT: Ashgate, 2004), 17.

74. For the Golden Rule, the Platinum Rule, and the Titanium Rule of the Jesus Commandment, see Leonard Sweet, *Postmodern Pilgrims: First Century Passion for the 21st Century World* (Nashville: Broadman and Holman, 2000), 126–28.

75. See C. D. C. Reeve's query that if to know God is to love God, why then is love a command? *Love's Confusions* (Cambridge: Harvard University Press, 2005), 2. Reeve also notes that we are *not* commanded to love God as we love ourselves,

only to love others as we love ourselves (14). Also see Zygmunt Bauman's observation: "Self-love is a matter of survival, and survival needs no commandments, since other (nonhuman) living creatures do very well without them, thank you. Loving one's neighbor as one loves oneself makes *human* survival unlike the survival of any other living creatures. Without that extension/transcendence of self-love, the prolongation of physical, bodily life is not yet, by itself, a *human* survival; is not the kind of survival that sets the humans apart from the beasts (and—never forget it—the angels). The precept to love one's neighbor challenges and defies the instincts set by nature; but it also challenges and defies the meaning of survival set by nature, and of that self-love which protects it." Bauman, *Liquid Love*, 78–79.

CHAPTER SIX

The epigraph for this chapter is taken from *Sayings of the Fathers, or, Pirke Aboth, the Hebrew Text, with a New English Translation and a Commentary*, by Joseph H. Hertz (New York: Behrman, 1945), 95. See also http://www.gutenberg.org/catalog/world/readfile?fk_files=26057&pageno=14.

1. See Deuteronomy 6:4–9.
2. See Deuteronomy 11:13–21.
3. Louis Jacobs, "Ekev," *Jewish Preaching: Homilies and Sermons* (Portland, OR: Vallentine Mitchell, 2004), 185.

4. Genesis 2:18, TNIV.

5. Actress Jamie Lee Curtis, quoted in Craig Wilson, "How Much Would Make You Smile," *USA Today*, 27 December 2004, http://www.usatoday.com/life/lifestyle/20041226money happiness_x.htm (accessed 11 April 2005).

6. William Maxwell, *So Long, See You Tomorrow* (New York: Alfred A. Knopf, 1980), 131.

7. John Mbiti, "The Contributions of Africa to the Religious Heritage of the World," Report Divine Love Retreat and Conference Centre, Enugu, Nigeria, 8–13 January 2001, World Council of Churches, http://www.wcccoe.org/wcc/what/interreligious/cd3714.html (accessed 19 August 2005). See also John Mbiti, *African Religions and Philosophy* (London: Heineman, 1969), 214.

8. John 10:30, KJV.

9. Luke 11:1.

10. My favorite definition of prayer comes from a husband-and-wife team: "two lovers sharing love together." See Mark and Patti Virkler, *Communion with God* (Shippensburg, PA: Destiny Image, 1990), 49.

11. 1 Corinthians 12:21.

12. Modernity was another name for disconnection. In a singleton society, everyone is alone and single. Even when we're together, we live singly together. In a singleton society, "freedom" means freedom from other people rather than freedom to do things with other people. In a singleton society, homes exist to protect us from one another, not to connect us to our neighbors and to our community. For more on "gated castles" and "gated com-

munities," see Gary Gumpert and Susan J. Drucker, "The Mediated Home in the Global Village," *Communication Research* 25, no. 4 (1998): 429.

13. For a variation and further rabbinic discussion of this quote, see *Tractate Berakhot,* trans. Jacob Neusner, *The Talmud of Babylonia I* (Chico, CA: Scholars, 1984), 409–11 [61A].

14. Gregory of Nazianzen, *Oratio* 40.41, quoted in Thomas F. Torrance, *Trinitarian Perspectives: Toward Doctrinal Agreement* (Edinburgh: T and T Clark, 1994), 26.

15. Quoted in Anouar Benmalek, *The Lovers of Algeria,* trans. Joanna Kilmartin (St. Paul, MN: Graywolf, 2004), [iii].

16. For an example of counterfactual reasoning, see *What Might Have Been: Leading Historians on Twelve "What Ifs" of History,* ed. Andrew Roberts (London: Weidenfeld and Nicholson, 2004).

17. Howard Gardner, *Changing Minds: The Art and Science of Changing Our Own and Other People's Minds* (Boston, MA: Harvard Business School Press, 2004), 263.

18. Genesis 12:1, KJV.

19. Louis Jacobs, "Lekh Lekha," *Jewish Preaching: Homilies and Sermons* (Portland, OR: Vallentine Mitchell, 2004), 35.

20. Genesis 4:9.

21. Arthur C. McGill's translation of Hebrews 13:3, *Death and Life: An American Theology* (Philadelphia: Fortress, 1987), 89.

22. 1 Corinthians 12:21.

23. 1 Corinthians 12:26.

24. Irving Singer, *The Nature of Love,* vol. 2, *Courtly and Romantic* (Chicago: University of Chicago Press, 1984), 195–205.

25. "No Man is an *Iland,* intire of it selfe.... Any Mans *death* diminishes *me,* because I am involved in *Mankinde; And* therefore never send to know for whom the *bell* tolls; It tolls for *thee.*" John Donne, [Meditation 17], *Devotions Upon Emergent Occasions, and Severall Steps in My Sicknes* (London: 1624), in John Donne, *Devotions Upon Emergent Occasions,* ed. Anthony Raspa (Montreal: McGill-Queens's University Press, 1975), 87.

26. Ecclesiastes 4:9–10.

27. Matthew 18:20.

28. If "two's company and three's a crowd," what's four and five? A revolution.

29. The exact quote is: "There is a wider abyss between two and three than between three and three million." G. K. Chesterton, *Alarms and Discursions* (New York: Dodd, Mead, 1911), 181, http://wikisource.org/wiki/Alarms_and_Discussions (accessed 21 August 2005).

30. This dialogue is from the 1964 movie *Zorba the Greek,* video recording. Screenplay by Michael Cacoyannis (Beverly Hills, CA: Twentieth Century Fox, 2004; adapted from Nikos Kazantzakis, *Zorba the Greek* (New York: Simon and Schuster, 1952), 13: "Like everyone else before me, I fell headlong into the ditch. I married. I took the road downhill. I became head of a family, I built a house, I had children–trouble."

31. In the well-known words attributed to Saint Teresa of Avila, "More tears are shed over answered prayers than unanswered ones." Quoted in James Campbell, "Homeless Houses: Cruelty,

Loneliness, and Love in the Art of Truman Capote," *TLS: Times Literary Supplement,* 5 November 2004, 4.

32. Listen to the words of fictional character Margaret Schlegel: "Only connect the prose and the passion, and both will be exalted, and human love will be seen at its height. Live in fragments no longer." E. M. Forster, *Howard's End* (New York: Book of the Month Club, 19–), 214.

33. John 11:35.

34. Mark 14:32–42.

35. John 2:13–17.

36. Just as love can be "sick," even a form of mental illness, so loving God can be "love sick." It is possible to have a romantic love of God that is of the mental-illness variety and doesn't last because it is based on the superficial and is prone to all sorts of diseases. A false understanding of intimacy is one of love-sick's greatest ports of entry.

37. Sara Churchwell, "Love at the Barre," *TLS: Times Literary Supplement,* 17 December 2004, 11.

38. Regina Barreca, *Perfect Husbands (and Other Fairy Tales): Demystifying Marriage, Men, and Romance* (New York: Harmony, 1993), 65.

39. This is the overarching theme of the thirteenth collection of Walter J. Burghardt's sermons, *To Be Just Is to Love: Homilies for a Church Renewing* (New York: Paulist, 2001).

40. One recent biography with a detailed index of Isaac Newton's discoveries is Patricia Fara, *Newton: The Making of Genius* (New York: Columbia University Press, 2002).

41. See Leonard Sweet, "The Revelation of Saint John and History," *Christianity Today,* 11 May 1973, 9–10.

42. Quoted in Petr Beckmann, *A History of Pi,* 2d ed. (Boulder, CO: Golem, 1971), 135.

43. Will L. Thompson, "Jesus Is All the World to Me" (1904), *Hymns of Praise Numbers One and Two Combined for the Church and Sunday School,* comp. F. G. Kingsbury (Chicago: Hope Publishing, 1926), 354.

44. Quoted in David Yount, *Celebrating the Rest of Your Life: A Baby Boomer's Guide to Spirituality* (Minneapolis, MN: Augsburg, 2005), 20.

45. Ephesians 5:2, NKJV.

46. Tennessee Williams, in his 1947 Pulitzer Prize–winning play, saw clearly that the desires of the heart shape our destiny. In the City of New Orleans, there is a place where the line of the streetcar named Desire intersects with the line of the streetcar named Cemeteries. To understand this is to understand it all. And for a completely different illustration of the effect of dreams and desire: ending extreme poverty in the world is not impossible, it's not expensive, and it's not hard. It just takes desire.

47. Thompson, "Jesus Is All the World to Me," 354.

48. "Each is drawn on by what delights him most." Virgil, *The Pastoral Poems: The Text of the Eclogues,* [Bk. 2, Line 65], trans. E. V. Rieu (Baltimore: Penguin, 1949), 35.

49. If memory serves, I think it was Simone Weil who first said this. But it also may be that I got this from a song by Mya,

"Fear of Flying," where she sings, "Love defies all gravity," http://www.lyricsfreak.com/m/mya/97213.html (accessed 18 August 2005).

50. Galatians 6:10.

51. So argues Victor Paul Furnish, *Theology and Ethics in Paul* (Nashville: Abingdon, 1968), 204.

52. Lorraine Kisly, *The Prayer of Fire: Experiencing the Lord's Prayer* (Brewster, MA: Paraclete, 2004), 91. Used by permission of Paraclete Press, www.paracletepress.com.

53. Kisly, *The Prayer of Fire*, 91.

54. François, Duc de la Rochefoucauld, *Réflexions ou Sentences et Maximes Morales* (Paris: Éditions Garnier Frères, 1961), 149; *Reflections and Moral Maxims* (Philadelphia: David McKay, [n.d.], 144.

55. James Fenton, "In Paris with You," *Out of Danger* (New York: Farrar Straus and Giroux, 1994), 13.

56. From "An Order for the Administration of the Sacrament of the Lord's Supper or Holy Communion II," *The Book of Worship for Church and Home...According to the Use of The United Methodist Church* (Nashville: Methodist Publishing, 1952), 383.

57. George Fox, "An Address to Friends in the Ministry," delivered at the Yearly Meeting, Third Month, 1658, at the House of John Cook, http://www.qhpress.org/quakerpages/qhoa/fox.htm (accessed 9 April 2005). See also *A Journal or Historical Account of the Life, Travels, Sufferings, Christian Experiences, and Labour of Love in the Work of...George Fox* (Philadelphia: Friends' Book Store), 299.

58. This is how Fox described the revelation: "Now the Lord God opened to me by His invisible power that every man was enlightened by the divine Light of Christ, and I saw it shine through all." *George Fox: An Autobiography*, ed. Rufus M. Jones (Philadelphia: Ferris and Leach, 1919), 101, http://www.strecorsoc.org/gfox/ch02.html (accessed 9 April 2005).

59. Quoted by Shane Claiborne of The Simple Way (Philadelphia). Dietrich Bonhoeffer's actual quote is, "Those who love their dream of a Christian community more than the Christian community itself become destroyers of that Christian community even though their personal intentions may be ever so honest, earnest, and sacrificial." *Life Together: Prayerbook of the Bible*, trans. Daniel W. Bloesch and James H. Burtness (Minneapolis, MN: Fortress, 1996), 36.

60. Elizabeth C. Clephane, "Beneath the Cross of Jesus," *Hymns of Praise Numbers One and Two Combined for the Church and Sunday School*, comp. F. G. Kingsbury (Chicago: Hope Publishing, 1926), 376.

61. J. Edward Chamberlin, *If This Is Your Land, Where Are Your Stories: Reimagining Home and Sacred Space* (Cleveland, OH: Pilgrim, 2003), 233.

62. Romans 7:19, NIV.

63. George Jones, "Wrong's What I Do Best," *Walls Can Fall* (Universal City, CA: MCA Records, 1992).

64. Neil Wyrick, "Dealing with Difficult People," *Ministry*, 74 (July 2001): 5–6.

65. See his visual riddle, "Ascending and Descending," M. C. Escher, *The Graphic Work: Introduced and Explained by the Artist* (New York: Barnes and Noble, 1996), 15 [plate 75].

66. Eighty-one-year-old Sumner Redstone, one of the richest people in the world, warns that every entrepreneur needs always to leave something on the table. He warns his colleagues never to let their competition leave the table feeling defeated: "A deal is good when it is good for both sides. If the other guy walks away as a loser, this ignores the fact that there is a life after the deal and we may need to work together again." Quoted in *American Way* (Dallas), 15 March 2005, 64.

67. "The Duck and the Grapes," in "Silly Bird Stories," *Bird Humor and Jokes,* http://www.cockatielcottage.net/giggles.html? (accessed 12 October 2005).

68. See Genesis 2:15.

69. Tim Richardson, "Earthly Paradises," *TLS: Times Literary Supplement,* 06 June 2003, 33.

70. Maureen Carroll, *Earthly Paradises: Ancient Gardens in History and Archaeology* (Los Angeles: The J. Paul Getty Museum, 2003), 83.

71. Psalm 24:1, KJV.

72. See Genesis 1:27–31; 2:7–9, 15–17.

73. David Petersen, *On the Wild Edge: In Search of a Natural Life* (New York: Henry Holt, 2005), 122.

74. D. H. Lawrence, *Sons and Lovers: Text, Background, and Criticism,* ed. Julian Moynahan (New York: Viking, 1968), 173.

75. Jared Diamond, *Collapse: How Societies Choose to Fail or Succeed* (New York: Viking, 2005), 79–111.

76. 1 John 4:19.

APPENDIX

The epigraph for this chapter is 1 Corinthians 9:22, NIV.

1. See Acts 4:12; Philippians 2:9–11.

2. See Acts 17:22–28.

3. 1 Corinthians 9:20, NIV.

4. For more on the discoveries of the human genome project, see "Only Connect," in "Survey: The Human Genome," *Economist*, 1 July 2000, insert, 8.

5. See 1 Corinthians 12:17–18.

6. Thomas O. Chisholm, "Great Is Thy Faithfulness," *Devotional Hymns: A Collection of Hymns and Songs for Use in All Services of the Church, Including Sunday School, Young People's Meetings, Missionary and Mid-Week Services* (Chicago: Hope Publishing, 1935), 46.

7. Acts 2:5, NIV.

8. Teresa of Avila, *The Interior Castle*, trans. Kieran Kavanaugh (New York: Paulist, 1979), 35, [I.1.1].

9. The book eventually became *The Far-Distant Oxus*, released in 1969.

10. Ransome went on to add: "As for the people who will eventually read your books, leave them to sort themselves. They don't concern you. All good books are *overheard.*" *Signalling from*

Mars: The Letters of Arthur Ransome, ed. Hugh Brogan (London: Jonathan Cape, 1997), 309.

11. Quoted in *Devotional Selections from George Matheson,* ed. Andrew Kosten (New York: Abingdon, 1962), 41.

12. See Peter Guralnick, *Last Train to Memphis: The Rise of Elvis Presley* (Boston, MA: Little, Brown, 1994) and Peter Guralnick, *Careless Love: The Unmaking of Elvis Presley* (Boston, MA: Little, Brown, 1999).

13. EPIC is an acronym standing for experiential, participatory, image-rich, and connective.

14. Kwame Anthony Appiah, *The Ethics of Identity* (Princeton, NJ: Princeton University Press, 2005), 213–72. For an excellent review of the significance of this book, see Jonathan Freedman, "A Rooted Cosmopolitan," *New York Times Book Review,* 12 June 2005, section 7, 16.

15. West Point cadets, at the same time they're learning home-sweet-home protection, must take pilgrimages to other cultures through year-long courses and required languages such as Chinese, Arabic, or Russian.

16. Rudyard Kipling, "The English Flag," *Collected Verse of Rudyard Kipling* (Garden City, NY: Doubleday, Page, 1920), 128. See also *Poetry of Rudyard Kipling, Full-Text,* http://www.everypoet.com/archive/poetry/Rudyard_Kipling/kipling_the_english_flag.htm (accessed 9 April 2005).

17. With thanks to Bruce Cook for this insight.

18. Elvis Presley also allegedly shot his television when Mel Torme or Frank Sinatra were singing. So it wasn't just Robert Goulet.

19. This was the theme of a sermon my mother, Mabel Boggs Sweet, preached on various occasions.

20. Appiah, *The Ethics of Identity,* 241.

21. See Philip Jenkins, *The Next Christendom: The Coming of Global Christianity* (New York: Oxford University Press, 2002), 2.

22. See Harry Emerson Fosdick, "God of Grace and God of Glory," *The United Methodist Hymnal: Book of United Methodist Worship* (Nashville: The United Methodist Publishing House, 1989), 577.

23. Quoted in Margaret Drabble, "Only Correct," *TLS: Times Literary Supplement,* 27 July 2005, 12–13.

24. 1 Thessalonians 4:16–17.

25. Revelation 22:20.

26. Cf. Matthew 28:19.

27. Mark 16:15, TNIV.

28. A people group consists of a "large ethnic or sociological grouping of individuals who perceive themselves to have a common affinity for one another." Fifty of these groups comprise half of the world's total population. Bill and Amy Stearns, *2020 Vision: Practical Ways Individuals and Churches Can Be Involved* (Minneapolis: Bethany, 2005), 179.

29. Stearns, *2020 Vision,* 180.

30. From the benchmark of 2005, forty-one years since Congress passed the Civil Rights Act that outlawed racial or sexual discrimination. In other words, it has taken us almost two thousand years to understand the meaning of "in Christ.... There is no longer slave or free, there is no longer male and female" (Galatians 3:26, 28).

31. Adam Kirsch, "Singing the Griot's Song," *TLS: Times Literary Supplement,* 15 October 2000, 10.

32. 1 Corinthians 13:12, KJV.

33. Ephesians 4:16, TNIV.

34. This key insight I learned from Andrew F. Walls, *The Cross-Cultural Process in Christian History: Studies in the Transmission and Appropriation of Faith* (Maryknoll, NY: Orbis, 2002), 67: "Cross-cultural diffusion has been necessary to Christianity. It has been its life's blood, and without it the faith could not have survived."

35. Revelation 7:9.

36. Stearns, *2020 Vision,* 182.

37. For more on this approach, see the upcoming book by Bob Roberts, founding pastor of NorthWood Church in Keller, Texas, *Transformation: How Glocal Churches Transform Lives and the World* (Grand Rapids, MI: Zondervan, 2006), GlocalNet: http://www.glocalnetresources.com/, NorthWood Church: http://www.northwoodchurch.org/index.html (accessed 22 August 2005).

38. "On that day Israel will be the third with Egypt and Assyria, a blessing in the midst of the earth, whom the Lord of hosts has blessed, saying, 'Blessed be Egypt my people, and Assyria the work of my hands, and Israel my heritage'" (Isaiah 19:24–25). For this quote and more on the significance of Isaiah 19, see Michael Nazir-Ali, "Culture, Conversation and Conversion: Some Priorities in Contemporary Mission," in *A.D. 2000 and Beyond: A Mission Agenda: A Festschrift for John Stott's 70th*

Birthday, ed. Vinay Samuel and Chris Sugden (Oxford: Regnum, 1991), 29.

39. Isaiah 49:6, NASB.

40. See John 2:1–11 and Luke 4:24–30, respectively.

41. For more on this see Bill and Amy Stearns, *2020 Vision: Amazing Stories of What God Is Doing Around the World* (Minneapolis: Bethany, 2005), 140.

42. Luke 2:32.

43. Acts 13:47.

44. See 2 Peter 3:12.

45. Revelation 5:9.

46. Matthew 24:14, NIV.

47. Quoted by James Romaine, "On a Clear Night, I Can See the Sun: Tim Rollins and K.O.S. Test Faith's Possibilities," *Image: A Journal of Arts and Religion* 45 (Spring 2005), 47.

48. Thomas Schmidt, *A Scandalous Beauty: The Artistry of God and the Way of the Cross* (Grand Rapids, MI: Brazos, 2002), 118–19.

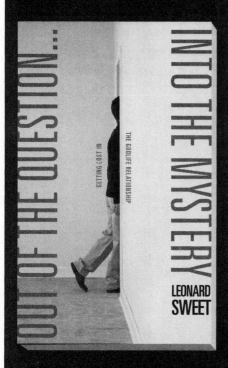

To learn more about WaterBrook Press and view
our catalog of products, log on to our Web site:
www.waterbrookpress.com

WATERBROOK
PRESS